The Golden Cage

By
Angela Tubb

First Published in Great Britain in 2015 by Tucann Books
Text & Images © Angela Tubb
All rights reserved
Design © TUCANN *Books*

No part of this publication may be reproduced or transmitted in any way or by any means, including electronic storage and retrieval, without prior permission of the publisher.

Isbn. 978-1-907516-35-1

Printed and bound by Tucann Design & Print, Unit 9, Blackthorn Way, Five Mile Business Park, Washingborough, Lincoln, LN4 1BF
tel;01522 790009 email tucannbooks@tucann.co.uk web. www.tucann.co.uk

Dedication

This book would not have been written without the support and encouragement of my second husband Adrian. He has always been there with love and understanding from the first time that we met. Always standing in the background, when I have been down he has lifted my spirits and taught me to enjoy life and live it to the full.

Angela at age 16 years

Chapter One

Do you wonder about what, would have happened in your life if you had made a different decision? Something quite simple like taking another train or not going to that party?
All through life we have to make choices and although we don't know it at the time, some of them can be life changing. I made such a choice and it took me on a journey for twenty two years.

Being asked by a post Graduate student *'if I would be his Pen Friend,'* seemed to me, to be a very simple question to which I answered yes. So the friendship on my side began. He told me he was twenty four years old, and had another eighteen months study in England before he would return to his own country - East Pakistan.

In our letter exchanges he told me about his family and his country.

We had studied Asia and India at school but I did not know anything about the politics of partition, when Pakistan had been created in 1947.

He told me about the Bay of Bengal and the wide rivers, making the land beautiful, green and fertile. The letters arrived at very regular intervals, all opening out to me a new world. I now had an older friend who had travelled half way round the world to complete his education.

I was sixteen, I had done quite well at school, but my mother had always hated school, she could not understand me loving school, so as soon as I was old enough to leave she got me a job in Marks and

Spencer's. In those days' boys and girls did what their parents told them, as my mother thought it a waste for a girl to have any further education, I went to work. I had wanted to go onto Art College and do a course in design. I had been going on a Saturday morning to Art College for the last two years and the Tutor said there was a place for me if my parents agreed. Mam said it would be a waste of time.

I have a brother Robert ten years younger, who was born when Mam was nearly forty, my parents wanted to be able to give him every chance.

One day a letter arrived and my new friend said he would like to come to York and see the City. Mam knew all about this pen friend, in fact she found his letters as interesting as I did. Mam and Dad invited him to come and stay with us for the next weekend.

We had a lovely time, York being such an interesting place, we could not see it all in two days.

We walked the walls of the City, then getting off them at Botham Bar we went to the Minster. Lunch in a restaurant was very grand for me, our family did not eat out, sometimes a cup of tea and a cake in a café, but then it had to be a special occasion.

After Lunch we went to The Treasurers house, walking round all the beautiful old buildings of St. Johns College, where I trained with the St. Johns Ambulance Brigade Cadets, every street in York was of interest to my friend. I was so happy to share my love of York with someone.

Onto St.Helens square, then the Mansion House, then the Shambles. We walked miles, very happy in each others company.

He went back to University, but two weeks later came for a second visit. This time he booked into a hotel in York, he said that he would visit our house to see my parents, maybe on the Sunday so that we could have a day together first.

That weekend he asked me to marry him. He told me that he loved me and wanted me to be his wife. My first reply was *'you will have to ask my Dad'*. He said he would most certainly ask my Father and asked me to tell my Dad that he would be coming to see him the next day, but not to tell him why.

We still did some sight seeing and I remember going up Clifford's

Tower and then to one of my favourite places the Museum Gardens. It was very romantic.

He had been to London to buy the ring, a large emerald with a diamond on either side, set in platinum. How did he know the right size? I then remembered he had tried my signet ring on his little finger, when he had been to see me last, but I had not thought anything about it.

He asked my father for my hand in marriage. My parents thought I was too young. My parents only objection was my age. They told us that we would have to wait until I was eighteen and then they would give their blessing to the match. This was far too long for my future husband; he was almost to the end of his study in England and was looking forward to his return to his own country.

We eloped to Scotland; when we arrived in Edinburgh we found accommodation in a Pakistani restaurant owner's house which overlooked Arthur's Seat. After visiting the Registry Office we went on day trips to pass the time until we were able to get married. When that happy day came I was still two months off my seventeenth birthday.

When we arrived at the Registry Office the police had caught up with us,.In the local York news paper it had been reported that I had been abducted. I told the police I had not been abducted, and of my own free will wanted to marry. The wedding went ahead.

We were married in the Registry Office of St. Giles, in Edinburgh, On the way to Waverley Station the next morning our marriage was in all the national news papers, in one, a photo had the caption *'Married life begins in a Police Box'*. We went back to England to face the music.

While we had been away the Yorkshire Evening Press had run the story and reported my Mother as saying *'The birds have flown'*, this became another head line. My mother had not told any of her relatives in Sunderland that I was missing, so it was at my Uncle Bens morning break, when he sat down to read his newspaper that he learnt all about it. After work instead of going home he went to Granny's to tell her. They were very cross with my Mother, as they had not been informed of the elopement, and they had never heard anything about my friendship with this young man.

Dad did look into my husbands back ground a little more and thought that I may never get a better offer. My Dad told me that if after going to East Pakistan, I found I could not stand it, Dad would bring me home.

From living in a small Yorkshire village, I would be living in Dacca, the capital of East Pakistan, with servants to look after me, this big adventure started because I said yes to being a Pen Friend.

At home in Yorkshire.

Chapter Two

'Wake up, wake up we are nearly there' I opened my eyes and saw that we were still in the plane. I had slept for the whole of my first flight.

The Air hostess came along and asked us to stay in our seats on landing. This was my first flight, in fact I had not been abroad until I got on the boat at Birkenhead for Karachi in West Pakistan.

The year was 1962 and the Dockers were on strike, our ship was to leave Liverpool, on the 30th March. My husband was taking me to his home in East Pakistan, we would stay on the ship as far as Karachi, after a short stay, we would fly the last leg to Dacca, the capitol of East Pakistan. This would be a flight over India as East Pakistan was on the Eastern side of India.

When we arrived for embarkation at the docks at Liverpool, we were told owing to the strike, we would be taken by coach through the new Mersey tunnel and get onto our ship, the 'Caladonia' at Birkenhead.

My husband said 'that means we won't have any cargo just our luggage in the hold'.

I understood the meaning of this when we got to the Bay of Biscay. One of the crew members was on deck at all times with a long sweeping brush. I had had some morning sickness early in my pregnancy but sea sickness was more persistent. I felt that the sea air would make me feel better, although it was quite windy I sat out on the deck, watching the sea heave and roll, it somehow made me feel a little better, until the man with the brush would have to clean the deck again with his long brush. He had hovered and waited as he knew what was coming next. Very few people were able to take meals, the dining room was deserted for about two days, things started to improve as we rounded the Rock of Gibraltar and got into the Mediterranean Sea, when the passengers finally came from their cabins, word got around the ship that the crew had also suffered with sea sickness. The 'Caladonia' was a one class ship belonging to the Anchor line, a small and compact ship and very friendly, mostly diplomats' going back to their post and tea planters with their family's returning after being home for Christmas and New year holiday.

The Anchor line publicity promoting a relaxing journey on the 'Caladonia' a one class ship

We stopped at Aden and went ashore; this was the first time I encountered an Eastern toilet. I was quite shocked; I had asked for the toilet but, one look, I declared 'I can't use that'. Calmly my husband told me that that was the style in his country so I would have to get used to it.

We went through the Suez Canal then across the Red sea and after three weeks reached Karachi.

The time at sea was very enjoyable, I saw dolphins for the first time, they were so friendly and swam alongside our boat, also Flying fish. When we went through the Suez Canal the GoliGoli man came on board to entertain us. He was an illusionist and showed us lots of magic tricks. Meanwhile our boat was surrounded by small craft all selling trinkets and leather goods. They passed the goods up to us to inspect, then the haggling would begin, if a price was agreed then the money went down to the vender in the basket. If not the goods were returned. Some times the goods went up and down in the baskets a few times until the bargaining was finished and a sale was made.

As we crossed the Red Sea we were getting nearer to our destination. Reaching Karachi we got off the ship, it was funny to be on land again, first we went into the large customs shed, Armed guards supervising the checking of Passports.

Finally we retrieved our luggage, the porters all competing with each other as to who would carry our suitcases, everything was so different, so much hustle and bustle it seemed that every one was shouting at each other.

Emerging from the Port we got a taxi, there was so much traffic, rickshaws, cars, people, animals all mixed up on the roads. The traffic police standing under his fixed umbrella, which shaded him from the fierce sun, he was blowing his whistle but still there did not seem to be any order or so it seemed to me. I was quite relived when we reached our hotel.

Standing at the door of the Hotel was the commissionaire, a huge man dressed in military fashion with a large moustache, on his head a beautiful fan shaped turban, this made him look seven foot tall. He came to attention and saluted us. Boys quickly came to carry our luggage and we were escorted to our room.

Cool calm well ordered service. This was a good start to my life in my husbands country.

Pakistan was still under Marshal Law with General Ayub Khan as President. Never experiencing Marshal Law I really did not know what it meant, but I was told that there was nothing to worry about as long as you stayed within the Law. The Army were in evidence every where.

We would be staying a week in Karachi; this was to enable me to get a new wardrobe of clothes. A visit to the tailor to be measured for blouses and petticoats, was first on the agenda.

The visit to the tailor was basically my husband and the tailor (Discussing, in Urdu), what I would need to start my eastern wardrobe. All the time the tailor was eyeing me up and down.

No tape measure used, I later learnt that they did not measure ladies, but I was assured that the blouses would be a perfect fit.

Six blouses in 'Lady Hamilton' silk in different colours plus six matching sari petticoats. All these items were delivered to our Hotel the following day and yes the blouses did fit perfectly. I had second thoughts about only having silk blouses, so while the Tailor was delivering the first order, I asked him to make me up, some more blouses in a fine lawn cotton material, again in different colours. Now I would be able to wear any sari I bought straight away.

Going into the Bazaar for Saris, this again was a new experience.

Shop keepers calling and inviting us into their shops. This trip took up most of one afternoon. The walls of the inside of the shop had shelving up to the ceiling on all sides, saris of every colour were neatly displayed in colour blocks, no counter but a platform area where the assistant sat cross legged, facing the front of the platform some easy chairs.

After greeting us, we were offered the comfortable chairs, the owner of the shop was sitting in the corner supervising the proceedings. After polite conversation in English, he established we had just arrived from England and on our way to East Pakistan, he asked what type of sari we were looking for, he took down sari after sari for my inspection.

If I mentioned a colour like 'Pink' down would come saris of every shade of pink. The saris would be piled up beside the shop owner who would be issuing instructions to his assistant. To help us with our choice we were offered tea and sweets. This was a very new way of shopping. I had decided that, when I met my in-laws I wanted to be in their traditional dress. We chose several saris, a mixture of silk and cotton ones. We took the purchases with us and went on to the next shop. Two pair of leather sandals and some pretty bangles later I thought by this time, I had spent more than enough money.

This was the first time I had shopped without thinking of the cost of anything. I didn't understand the money and my husband said it was alright for now, and that we could soon buy more when we reached Dacca.

I didn't sleep very well on the last night in Karachi as I was so excited, this was my first flight. We were going in a Boeing 747.

Now they were waking me, I had slept the whole way.

After most of the passengers had got off the plane, the hostess came and readjusted my sari for me, making sure the pleating at the front of the skirt were hanging correctly, she checked my lipstick and hair, when she was happy with me, she then escorted us to the door of the plane. I was pleased that I had worn a sari a few times in England, when some of the Indian girl students from the University had helped me by showing me how to put one on.

You could feel the heat from the tarmac, this was a hot spicy humid heat, it was the smell of the sub-continent, going down the steep steps I could see a group of people waiting for us at the end of a red carpet. My husband was waving and calling Ba-Ba, Ma, after five years he was over joyed to be back home.

Chapter three

After our Welcome at the Airport we were whisked away in a Flower decorated car.

I had never seen a Bengali style wedding car before, but that's what it was. The car was completely covered with garlands of sweet scented Jasmine flowers, and strings of Marigolds, only a tiny space left in the windscreen for the driver to see the way. As I already had at least four garlands about my neck, the perfume was very strong, and sweet. The roads were lined with beautiful Bougainvillea trees all brilliantly coloured the walls lining the road were white washed and although the road was dusty it had a clean and ordered feeling to it. We were travelling through the Cantonment Area.

We travelled into the new part of Dacca city and soon arrived at the bungalow my in-laws had rented for us. My mother-in-law explained (through an interpreter) that they had only purchased the very basic furniture, so that when I was ready, I could complete the furnishings of the house to my own taste, I thought this was very thoughtful and certainly a good start to our relationship.

The same with the servants, they had only been hired on a short term basis, so that I could change things if I wished. As I did not know the language I thought it would be a good idea to go quite carefully at first and not to make changes unless really necessary. Soon I settled into my new life.

I remember my first morning in Dacca. A male servant arrived from my next door neighbour. He was immaculately dressed, all in white, carrying a tray covered with a white lace cloth. He told my husband 'I have brought Memsahib's breakfast, it is welcome gift from the lady who lives next door'. Uncovering it with a flourish it was beautifully presented, first a bowl of cornflakes 'fresh cows milk memsahib' then a perfectly boiled egg with toast 'from bazaar this day Memsahib' then toast and marmalade and a pot of tea. The servant was so attentive I think if I had asked him to feed me he would have. This was something I would have to get used to, but at first I did feel a little shy eating while they attended to my every need. The lady next door became a good friend, as she had just returned from a holiday in London, she knew I would be more comfortable having an English breakfast rather that the Bengali roti and potato bhaji which is normally eaten for breakfast.

We invited my mother-in-law to stay in Dacca with us and not return to her own house in Khulna. I felt that I would like to have someone at home when my husband went to his office, also the language was a problem and you can only get so far with sign language. She very happily stayed while my father-in-law who could speak very good English travelled back and forth looking after his interests in Khulna.

My father-in-law had been a high ranking police officer in British India, in charge of a District; he retired about six months before partition in 1947. After partition with all the unrest the new East Pakistan government requested that he come out of Retirement and take up his old post. He served the East Pakistan Government for a further ten years and finally retired at the age of seventy six.

As I was having my first baby I booked in to the Holy Family Hospital, this hospital was run by an order of American nuns. Baby was due in September so I had a lot of hot weather to get through, plus the monsoon.

My mother-in-law soon had vegetables growing in the garden and Golden Marigolds lined the pathway up to the front Veranda.

How can I describe the heat? As the sun arose the heat would wrap its self around you- before breakfast I would take a shower, what delight, cold water so soothing for the Prickly heat. About two hours later I would be ready for my next shower and so it would go all through the day, I was showering as many as five times a day.

I was looking forward to Monsoon, What I didn't understand

was that Monsoon is so humid. Evening time we would take a ride on a Rickshaw, the cool evening breeze was wonderful. We would visit friends and family. One family we would visit lived in old Dacca. There they didn't have electricity and the rooms were lit with oil lamps. This was the home of a distant uncle who also happened to be the National Poet. His household was unusual as he only had daughters and when they married he could not bear the thought of them leaving home so he had the son-in-laws move into his house.

This household was an intellectual, artistic family and I do remember some of the children's names such as Sonnet and one boy called Keats.

All being highly educated, conversation with them all was no problem, music played a big part of this families life also Classical singing, this was my first introduction to beautiful Indian music both sung and played. They could all play so many instruments. I always enjoyed my visit to them. Not so much the area where they lived. To get there we had to go into the old town, very narrow streets with an open drain on one side, just enough space to get a rickshaw down. On my first visit I noticed an array of brightly coloured saris hanging down into one of the side streets with dilapidated buildings on each side, as I had not seen anything like this before I asked what was down that road. 'The red light Area' next question 'What is a red light Area? I had no idea that such a place existed.

Uncle lived about another half mile further on into the old Dacca. Many very old, wealthy families lived in this part of Dacca and the buildings were very beautiful and ornate, large veranda's, mosaic floors and flat roofs where the children played or flew kites.

My Bungalow was in the newer part of the City. I soon got used to sleeping under a mosquito net and hear the hum of the electric fan. Every sound was new, the buzzing of the mosquitoes, the howls of the jackals, the hooting of the car horns, people talking in the road, someone singing, babies crying all life was there in the night.

When you don't understand a language every thing can be very mystifying, I was making progress with the Bengali language. Along the way I made mistakes, simple words would get miss pronounced and mean something very different to what I was trying to say. Many years later after my return to England I had students from the language school lodge with me. I could feel for them when they tried to understand the difference between ship and sheep. In the early days in Dacca I was trying to tell someone about a certain street, but in the telling it changed into a bucket.

Life settled into a routine. My mother-in-law was always there to help me, she was so looking forward to our new baby. Her first Grandchild.

My husband (being a man) had not told me about the things I wouldn't find in Dacca, many things I was used to, were just not available.

Fortunately sewing was a joy to me and so I made baby clothes for the baby, then I found out that nappies were unheard of. Well a baby without a nappy just was not on. Soft fine cotton material was bought and I hem stitched twenty four squares and made my own nappies for baby. I got my mother to send me the nappy pins from England. Due to the heat I always seemed to have an upset tummy, as my tummy got bigger I lost weight, also I suffered from Prickly heat even having it on the soles of my feet.

.

Old Dacca street scene.

Mary Age 3

Solomon Age 6

Chapter Four

Two months after my eighteenth Birthday I gave birth to a healthy baby boy. I was a good wife in Bengali eyes to have a first born baby boy. He was not a good baby, crying all night seemed to be normal for him, after many sleepless nights which my husband complained about, 'as he had to go to work' my mother-in-law took charge each night at about eleven o'clock until early morning. In the morning I would play with him while Ma had some rest. As a first time Mum I couldn't understand what I was doing wrong. I wanted to breast feed my baby, but mother-in-law said she thought baby was perhaps hungry, so we introduced Glaxo. I must admit it did help, then I found out that also a dummy was given to him at night, that was something that I didn't like, but anything for a bit of peace, so baby won in the end.

    There was another English girl living quite close to us, and I would go over to visit her in the day time, before our husbands came back from the office, her name was Jean. She was married to another Pakistani Engineer, they had been married for about eight years. She was not as 'lucky' as me as she had three little girls and another baby on the way. From what she told me about her in-laws (who lived in West Pakistan) they wanted a grandson and so they were not happy with her having only girls up to now. As her husband's job was in Dacca they did not have a lot of contact with his family. She missed England very much and as Jean was an only child she came from a very small family and missed her mother. My arrival was good for her as we lived quite near to each other and we could pop round to see each other, just for a cup of tea and a natter. She had a teacher to help her with her Urdu. Pakistan at that time had Urdu and Bengali as first languages and English as Second language.

When Bambino was about six months old we started to have better nights, but as he spent such a lot of time awake he was talking very early. I learnt my first few words of Bengali from him. As most of the family were Bengali speakers I chose to have a tutor of Bengali to teach me. My tutor was a Hindu Brahmin he came each afternoon, Monday to Friday for a two hour lesson. I can see him now in my minds eye, marching up the road wearing a spotless dhoti and long white granddad shirt. He also had a long tail of hair which he plaited from the crown of his head. He was clean shaved and wore Glasses. I called him Sir. Having been educated in British India his English was very correct, if not a little old fashioned, but without a very heavy accent. The first lessons were spent holding a mirror as he insisted, it was where, I put my tongue depended on what sound I made with my mouth. After that came the sounds to be made from the different parts of the throat.

He taught me well, when (many years later) my young grandsons came to visit me in England they thought I had a very posh way of speaking Bengal, this was because I don't use any slang words, and spoke Bengali correctly. Life settled into a pleasant time of visiting lady friends maybe going to play bridge in the Mornings, some of the ladies also played tennis in the cooler season or we would have a swimming party, just sitting around a pool having cool drinks.

One of my favourite drinks was green coconut water, I found it most refreshing after a swim. When my husband came home from the office, at about two o'clock he would sometimes bring a car from the office. While I studied with Sir, he would take some rest and a shower then we would go into the centre of Dacca, maybe to the Dacca Club for the evening. This used to be called the Gymkhana Club and was a left over from the Raj, very Edwardian in a way. The first time I went there the Bar attendant came and asked me if I had an Alcoholic Licence, as I didn't drink I said no. He was so disappointed, we then learnt that when foreigners came into a 'Dry' country such as East Pakistan they could declare themselves an Alcoholic, they would get a licence to drink. The

Bar tender said that was how he was able to run his bar with all the Alcoholics licences. Other times we went out on a Cycle Rickshaw or a Tuk-tuk which in Dacca are called Baby Taxi's.

When I lived in England I had only been to the cinema a very few times, our church the Elim Evangelical Church, did not approve of the Cinema, but now in Dacca we went almost every week. The Naz cinema showed only English films and was in the same building as my favourite Chinese Restaurant. We didn't keep an Ayah for the Baby as he always had his grandmother to look after him when we went out. She loved him so much, she had only the one child, my husband, which is quite unusual in Asia, she loved children, she encouraged us to go out. When one of our nieces came for a visit she wanted to stay, she was a big help and also a companion for my mother-in-law. Then a young cousin came and he wanted to stay, soon our Bungalow was getting too small for us all. My father-in-law being quite elderly was travelling back and forth from Khulna to Dacca on the river steamer called 'The Rocket'. This was something again left over from the Raj, a paddle steamer which looked very much like the ones seen on the Mississippi river.

The First Class cabins were on the top deck, they surrounded a Grand dining room, an open sun deck at the front with steamer chairs to relax on and watch the beautiful scenery as you drifted by. White clad attendants called bearers were always on hand to pander to the First Class passengers every need.

Below on the open deck the Deck Class passengers would be crowded in, not only people but all their belongings, sometimes they would be moving house, they would have all their house hold goods too. Plus chickens and the odd animal or two. On the open deck mosquito nets would be strung up, making little rooms, ladies then had some privacy. Children would be running around and generally a lot of noise. Some times while some of the local steamers were loading at the Dacca passenger Ghat one would think 'they can't get any more on', and some of the smaller craft did over load, some times nasty accidents would happen. The Rocket was a daily service from Dacca to Khulna and also a bit more costly, we always used it as we thought it was safer as they kept the numbers down.

As we were running short of room in our Dacca home, my father-in-law on his visits now took to sleeping on the veranda, in hot weather this is the place of choice for the men, but winter was coming on and not ideal for an elderly Gentleman.

We looked at other houses, but nothing seemed to be right. Always my husband compared them to the house he had built for himself, before going to England. Only problem was it was in Khulna, my husband had said from time to time he would like to have his own business, we would have to decide when the time was right to do this, if we moved to Khulna we had our own house and land for such a project. I had formed new friends in Dacca, many were foreigners and their wives and this was a very mobile group. Moving to Khulna I could make friends on a more permanent basis. Khulna was a District Town two hundred miles from Dacca. Near to Khulna was the Port of Chalna and the rain forest of Sundarbans and the River Delta going into the Bay of Bengal.

After two years in Dacca we moved to Khulna.

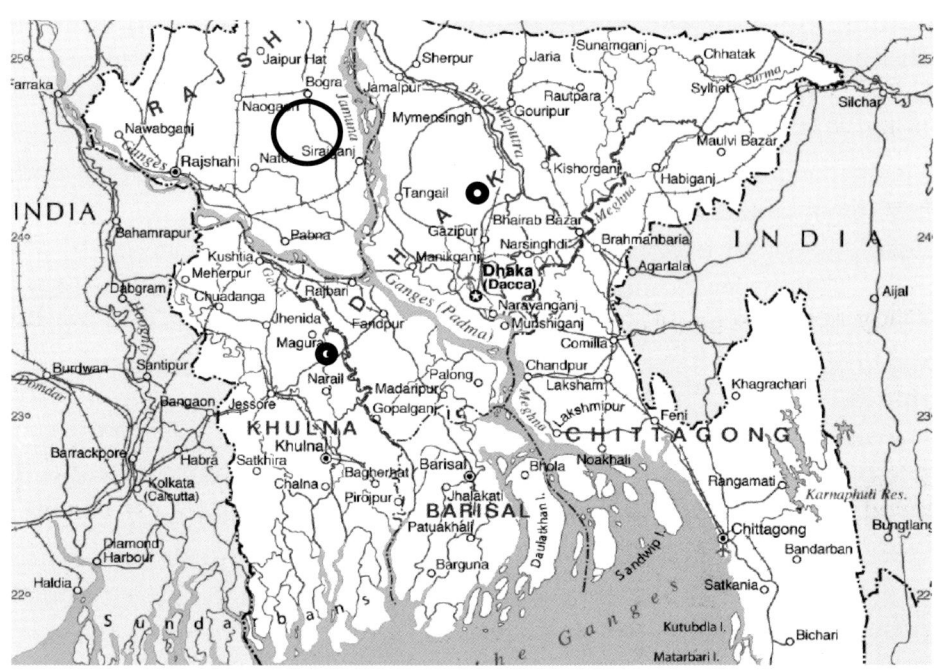

Map showing the position of Dacca and Khulna. Circled is the district of PABNA where we had the village home on the banks of the Ganges

Chapter Five

Some thing might happen or I hear some news and it triggers a memory. When we had an eclipse of the sun it reminded me of my Mother-in-law. She was always ready to protect me, she would tell me all the 'old wives tales' of Bangladesh and some i think from India. Although a devout Muslim she had some knowledge of Hindu Mythology, all mixed up together there was some very strange things to avoid and to observe. Although I am not superstitious myself, not to upset Ma I would go along with her to keep her happy, it was another thing in private.

The eclipse was the sun being eaten by a dragon; Ma would insist that during the time of the eclipse, we were not to eat or drink anything. I don't know the reasoning why but I do remember Ma would be on guard to make sure we didn't eat or drink. Also if there was a chance of a lady being pregnant, the lady would go to her room and close all the windows and shutters, then firmly bolt the door and wait until the sun had reappeared. Then she would be told it was 'all clear'. Supposedly this protected her unborn child from some deformity.

When I went to Dacca I was already pregnant with my first child, I loved fruit and, with so much fresh fruit around I happily eat banana, mango, papaya, passion fruit and litchis, but I was not allowed to eat pineapple by Ma, she thought that if I ate pineapple I would miscarry.

Another fruit I did not eat for quite a few years was Jack fruit. When the British sailors came to any port in the Bay of Bengal they were forbidden to eat Jack fruit by their Commanding Officers. The reason for this was that it has a laxative effect, and although it is truly delicious, just like a fragrant custard in taste, it made the sailors ill.

Jack fruit is a fruit to be shared, a Jack fruit can't be hidden from other people in the house as it has such a strong distinctive smell, it has a very rough outer skin, and one whole Jack fruit could weigh up to a stone in weight. Once broken open there are individual fruits with a stone inside each one. After eating two or three of these yellow individual fruits you feel quite satisfied. The local people keep the stones out of the fruits, they can be used as a vegetable in a curry. Another way is to chop them up and fry them with onion, garlic and green chillies and serve as a side dish for white rice. The only thing to throw away is the hard outer skin. Ma was of the strong belief that, what a nursing mother ate, had an effect on the baby, again restrictions came into force. A long list would be announced by Ma such as, no hot spices, no prawns and ice cream were out. Also many other things which would cause baby to have colic, upset tummy, hiccups, runny nose or cough.

By now I knew enough Bengali to introduce Ma to some of our methods so I introduced her to Woodwords Gripe Water, I don't think you can get it now, but once Ma had agreed to give it a try she was instantly converted. I think the sale of Gripe Water went up in our area, as she was telling all how wonderful it was. I did catch her once giving it to my father-in-law, when he had wind.

Ma strongly believed that if pigeons nested in a property that it was a sign of happiness and good fortune for the family who lived there. She would go onto the flat roof of our home and put out grain for them to feed, always saying the little they ate would come back to us in abundance. We had a dove cote made and she was so delighted to see the pigeons nesting, daily she brought the reports, first about the eggs then the chicks. In some parts of the world pigeon is eaten but it is something I will never eat.

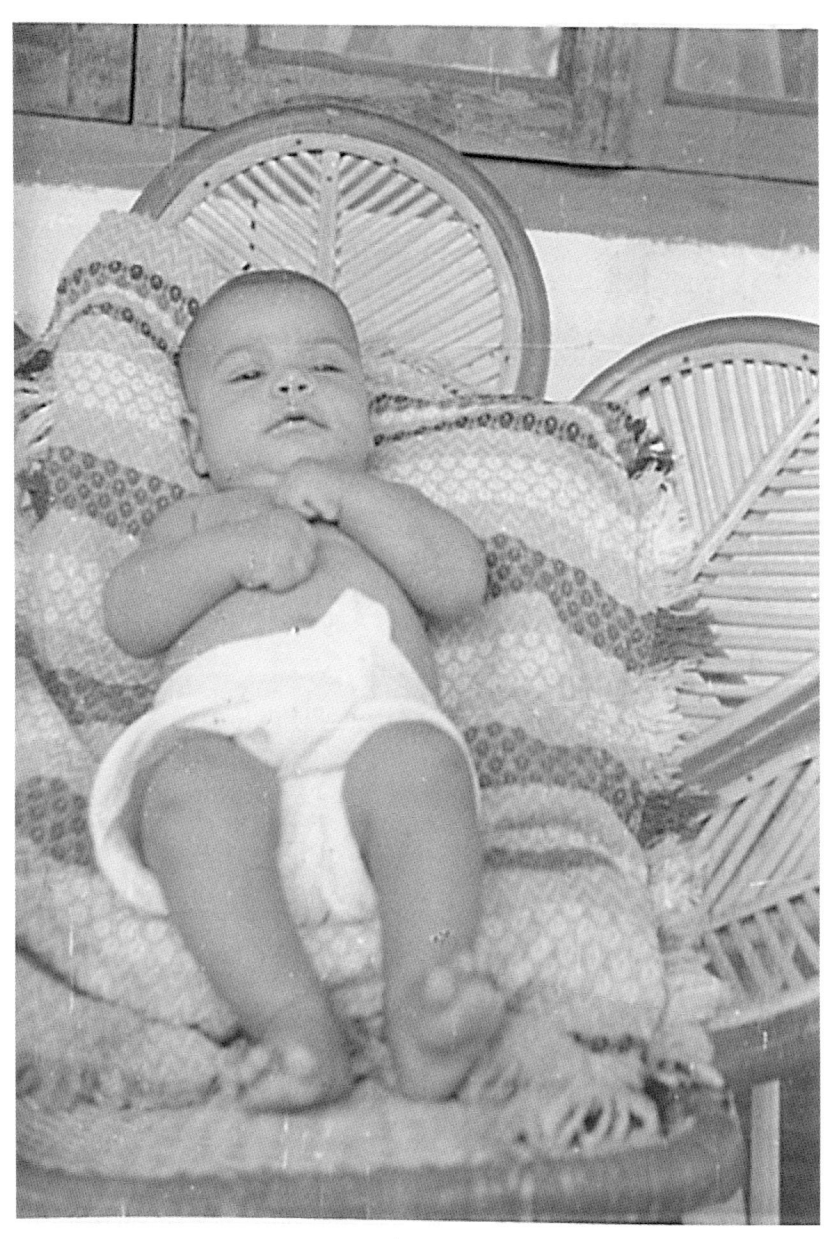

Solomon 4 months old

Chapter Six

My mother and father-in-law, were married when my mother-in-law was sixteen, but for many years they were childless and almost gave up on the thought of having a baby. In this situation in their culture, it is acceptable for the husband to take another wife, my father-in-law chose not to, after about twenty five years of marriage they had a baby son. After such a long time childless it was a great joy for them. This was my husband.

After Graduating as an Engineer my husband went to work as an Engineer in the Local shipyard but he also applied for a scholarship to come to study in England. He won the scholarship and that is how we met. When I first went to East Pakistan I had so much to learn about their customs, traditions, food and how to cook it, everything was so different. I got used to eating rice, and as fish was mostly eaten I soon got to know the taste of the different fish. Even Bread had a different taste, how I yearned for a nice slice of English bread with butter and Jam.

With the help and guidance of my mother-in-law settling into my new life was not too difficult. I soon got used to calling her Ma and she really was like a mother to me. She taught me everything. She couldn't speak a word of English. When she was a young girl (even in a well to do family) girls were not educated and as a result she could not read or write. At the same time she was a very intelligent and a very loving lady. Ma had a very sweet and gentle way of speaking and she would talk to me in Bengali. I did not understand but after some time it is possible to pick up the rhythm of the spoken word and a certain comprehension comes to you.

As confidence grew I tried to speak to her and without realizing it I was able to communicate. I understood new words every day and with encouragement from every one in the household, I started to speak Bengali. This was a huge help in the running of the house and with the servants. Now I could understand more, I had an idea of what was going on. When Ma went out visiting she always took me with her, I was the daughter she had never had. Introductions to anyone new were 'this is my daughter' this made me feel wanted, so the settling down into my new life was quite easy. Ma did everything to help me, after the baby arrived she was so happy, any thoughts of her going back to live in her own house were out of the question.

As we got on so well this suited me, the house was mine and everyone always asked me first regarding the daily running of the house, the staff would always refer to me but I knew Ma was there in the background ready to help and give me advice. On my arrival at Dacca airport Ma had placed around my neck a chain and locket as a welcome to the family. As I was English she had not been too sure of what type of jewellery I would like. She had decided on a Gold locket and chain, the locket was star shaped set with a diamond in the centre, a ruby was set at each point of the star. It was very beautiful. The chain was very useful as I could change lockets and have a different necklace. After the birth of my baby she gave me Gold bangles as a gift for giving her a Grandson. We lived together until her death. After she died I always felt she was watching over me and if I had a problem, sitting down quietly and thinking of her always seemed to help me find a solution.

Chapter Seven

Working as Chief Engineer in the Cotton Mill in Khulna, my husband was not utilizing the five years post graduate Engineering he had studied in England. Foreign Aid was waiting to be applied for to bring Electricity to every one in East Pakistan. Some of our friends were already working in this field but there was no Bengali run engineering companies, all were foreign companies employing Bengalis. This was an ideal time to set up our own Electrical and Mechanical Engineering Company. We had put another wing onto our house, so we had enough room to have our Head office. The office had to look business like and efficient. We made a separate entrance to the office, so that business visitors would not be coming through our main house gate or gardens. Among our extended family was a young man who had trained as a Stenographer but not yet found a job. We took him on as Typist and PA. We also hired an office peon. (an Indian name for a person who does odd jobs) This was all done on speculation.

Soon we got our first Contract. Technical drawings were made by my husband, but any tracing work I would do. We submitted Tenders for the rural electrification of different parts of East Pakistan.
The first one was for a small town about forty miles from where we lived. We won the tender, now we needed workman, a Foreman and maybe a site Engineer. Putting our money together we bravely hired our staff. Most of the workers came from Pabna district where my father-in-law had a lot of farm land. As the work got underway the men were

eager to learn, they worked hard. Electricity was a new thing for every one. Only the two main roads in Dacca where the Government Offices and High Court buildings were had electricity and roads into the new housing area near to Dacca Airport. We soon had a very highly trained work force. As one job was completed another was awarded to us. That meant that I had to keep an eye on the post, and be able to make sure that all the deadlines for submitting tenders were met. Keep an eye on the books, and also make sure that bills were paid on time, and that banking was done correctly. My husband would be out on site inspections, as the company grew this got too much for me, I had a very busy house hold and a growing family. We could now afford to hire an accountant and more graduate engineers.

Within five years the company had grown to employ over two hundred skilled and semi-skilled workers with ten officers. Being a local company our quotes for the work always came below the foreign companies so we got a lot of work sometimes as many as three sites would be working at a time.

During this time I had to go to Dacca for the birth of our second child a little girl, we called her Mary. I went to the Holy Family again, travelling to Dacca when I was six months pregnant. Some minor complication meant that I needed to be close to the hospital, and at seven months pregnant I was hospitalised. It was while I was in the Holy Family Hospital that Pakistan had the six days war with India.

The British high commissioners wife came to see me and said that all British citizens were being evacuated. She wanted me to go with them, but only up to Singapore where they would book me into the hospital. As I was by now close to having my baby, I felt safer in the hospital in Dacca. So I stayed in the Holy Family Hospital. My friend Nan had come to Dacca with her husband Duncan, after her departure, which I later found out was not without drama, Duncan called in to the hospital before making the journey back to Khulna where he worked in the Shipyard as a keel layer. The six days war was over so quickly but it took ages for my friend to get back to her husband Duncan.

On her return from Scotland she told me about their evacuation. Mostly Women and children would be getting onto the transport plane which was being provided to get them out which was organised by the

British Government. On leaving the Airport building they were under fire and they had to run to the plane.

The transport plane was not comfortable and already some of the ladies were having second thoughts and wishing they had waited to see what would happen. When they arrived in Singapore, the British evacuees were billeted in Nissan huts, not the hotels which they had expected. There they stayed until regular flights could be booked for them to take them to Great Britain.

As their departure from Dacca had all happened in a hurry and having been told hand luggage only it was a very difficult time, August in Asia is hot. Afterwards hearing all of this from my friend Nan, I knew I had taken the right choice by staying in the hospital at Dacca. In this hot and sometimes alien environment I had been safer with the American Nuns. I was by myself in Dacca as my husband had his business to look after and he knew I was safe in the Hospital. I had my own room with a veranda leading on to well tended lawn. I would watch the gardeners at their work, squatting to cut the grass by hand, no lawn mowers, just a small sharp curved knife. Jasmin and golden marigolds gave colour to the gardens, Also the beautiful Bougainvillea trees which stood along the road side edge of the hospital. One other girl was a lady in waiting like me, she was a Tea planter's wife and had come from Syhlet for the birth of her first baby.

I would sit on my veranda and watch the fighters go off and then count them back in. Myra had her baby first, it was a little girl. Her husband didn't get to Dacca for the birth. My husband arrived just in time for the arrival of his baby daughter, he did not attend any of the births, it wasn't the done thing and I most certainly did not want him to be present. At six days old we took baby Mary home, travelling in a helicopter. The pilot asked the age of the child and when I said six days he decided to fly very low, it seemed as if we only just skimmed the tops of the trees and also there was a lot of vibration. The flight attendant asked me to place my hands over Mary's ears for the duration of the flight. She slept all the way only opening her eyes on landing, where she was met by her brother.

Chapter Eight

With my son who was three years old and baby sister, our family was growing, so was the household, and when we decided to go for a long vacation to the ancestral village home in Pubna district, the things we had to take seemed to be endless. Basic things were there in the village house, but with young children you can never travel light.

I had lots of help, and so bedding, crockery, cutlery, and personal items were all assembled by the different helpers, we would take the whole household and go to Nazirjang for a Month in November. When the monsoon rains have finished and the last of the really hot weather is over, Bangladesh is green with a very comfortable temperature ideal for relaxation. This was my first trip on a train in Bangladesh. We had booked the whole of a First Class Carriage, this enabled our party to stay together, for the overnight journey.

The train left Khulna at 9 o'clock in the evening. The Children were already sleepy and so we put them to bed, they loved the bunks. As the bunks were already made up for us we did not need to open any of our luggage. The train moved very slowly out of Khulna Station. The movement of the train was different to the trains in England. We had eaten our Evening meal before leaving home. The attendant brought us snacks and cool drinks.

Soon we all settled down for some rest. As there wasn't enough bunks for every one, the helpers in our party had bed rolls which were rolled out in the seated area of our Carriage, so every one had somewhere to sleep. The train seemed to stop and start quite a bit and never reached any high speed. We trundled on through the night. Finally we got to our Station very early the next morning. The station was already very crowded, as I later learned that our train was the only train for 24 hours, stopping at that station.

Getting down from the train we were met by the boatmen from the village, our nephew had brought our breakfast with him so we ate before going to the boats. The usual Bengali breakfast of Vegetable Bhaji wrapped in a roti. Very strong tea was brought for us from the tea stall at the Ghat. Waiting for us at the Landing stage was a long narrow country boat, no outboard motor just man power, to take us across the mighty fast flowing Ganges River, which at this point was said to be about twelve miles wide. This being Bangladesh we did not have life Jackets.

When we finally arrived on the other side of the river. News of our arrival had reached far and wide, and although the villagers had heard about me, (the English lady) they all came to see for themselves. By this time I had been in this country long enough to cope with people and children coming to have a look, this was now normal.

Our house was on the banks of the river, it was built in traditional style of an Indian Bungalow. Built on a large platform of earth, the construction was of corrugated tin, with a wide veranda on all sides, Wooden doors and windows with bars and louvered shutters. The floor seemed to be highly polished , this had been achieved over many years, cow dung and water mixed and then plastered daily, when dry a lovely smooth floor shining and looking like Mahogany.

Entering into the one room there was some large wooden chairs, carved and with arms and high backs, an iron safe, a large metal trunk and a bed. I say bed, it was huge. At least 8 foot square, with a high head board beautifully carved, a railing 18 inches high surrounded the bed with, a little gate at one side, to enable you to get up and in to the bed. This was a real old fashioned family bed, made in solid teak. Each leg of the bed was standing on its own little earthen container, which had a trough containing water. This was to stop ants and any other creepy crawly's from climbing up on to bed. Soon the bedding was brought in and the bed made up, a mosquito net was attached to the beautifully carved four posts at each corner of the bed, it looked very grand and also looked very comfortable. No curtains at the windows, but when we opened the shutters we had a lovely cool breeze coming off the River. Evening time the hurricane lamps would be lit, these villages did not have electricity at this time. I kept a lamp lit in the room all night.

  Food would be prepared in a small thatched hut, far enough away so that we would only get the aroma, not the smoke from the earthen wood fire that never seemed to go out. My Father-in-law had gone a few days ahead and had spent his time having his men constructing a bathroom and toilet for us. I shall try to describe the toilet. A pit about 5 feet deep had been dug; across it two stout bamboos had been placed with about 9 inch gap. For privacy four bamboos had been placed around the pit to make an enclosure, the bamboos having heavy duty hessian nailed to them. One side piece had a loop to hang over the top of the bamboo, this was the door. Water would be carried in an earthen pot, by my ayah, who would shoo off the children or any onlookers and I would be escorted to this 'toilet'. While I was inside this custom made enclosure my ayah would stand guard. With good balance I had to place one foot on each of the horizontal bamboos, and aim between the bamboos.

  The bathroom was another of my father-in-laws designs. It was a small thatched hut with no windows and one door. Ayah would bring from the river, large quantities of water and pour them into half an oil drum. Hanging from the rafters was a contraption for a shower. This was a large ghee tin with small holes made in the base, ayah was to stand on a stool and pore water into the ghee tin, I would stand under the ghee tin and have a shower. Have you ever had the feeling you are being watched? I was having my shower and I had this uneasy feeling. Looking at the woven walls of my bath hut, I could see that there were some small holes and at each hole an eye. Ayah soon chased them off. I also dispensed of my ayah's help and used a large mug to pour the water over myself, I gave her the duty of guard outside.

Chapter Nine

My time in the village house was so relaxing. When we had first arrived my every movement was noted and observed, but as I got more used to them being there watching and reporting on me, it seemed to be quite normal. I must say I was never lonely. Early morning after cleaning my teeth (in public so it seemed) I would have a cup of tea pored from my small Old Country Rose teapot. Tea made in an East Pakistani Village was made in a large urn and stewed until it is very black, the milk added and then boiled up, this makes a dark thick sickly drink, nothing like the tea we drink. Sometimes they would add Molasses for sweetening. After my cup of tea I would wander to the river bank and watch the sunrise, the Fishermen would be out on the river with their large triangular nets. If they caught a nice big fish they would give it to one of the many children to take home it would be cooked by the time they returned from the river. My father-in-law would be found down there too, he also would wait until a fish was caught to his fancy, purchase it from the fisherman and have it sent home for his breakfast. Making our way back to the house we could see the cows being milked and every one getting ready for another day.

After breakfast I could wander off with the company of most of the village children to see people at their daily work. In the next small hamlet lived a potter. He controlled the wheel with his feet, clay would be brought from the river bank, he would kneed it to make it smooth then throw a lump onto the wheel. As if by magic a pot would

be created. He put the made pots onto a tray to be placed in the sun to dry.
This potter didn't have a kiln so the pots he made were to be used once, then thrown away. I understood that each potter had his own niche in the market, if a potter could make a kiln fired with wood, he could then make pots suitable for carrying water. Some villages only had earthen pots even for cooking, so the potter made a good living and would be able to send his children to school.

The women were always busy, cleaning rice and cooking. In the afternoon they would make rice cakes or sweet dishes. To make a rice cake first the rice must be ground into flour, Two large grinding stones would be used, and as there was no electricity the girls would grind by hand. The older women would be in charge of the batter mixing and they would cook the cakes in special trays, very much like our small cake trays but again these were made of clay. After the cakes were cooked they then would be soaked in a sweet juice. After about an hour the cakes would have swelled up to double their original size. A bit like Rum Baba's but with out the rum. One of the sweet dishes which the ladies made, was with pastry made from the rice flour, cut into small circles, sweetened coconut would be put onto the pastry and sealed. It would look just like a miniature pasty, then the pasty was deep fried in Ghee.

My son enjoyed going with the other little boys to watch the cows, just wandering around with a nice stick seemed to be his heaven. No tractor here, but he could stand on a ladder while the oxen walked round in a circle threshing the rice. The ladies would then come and winnow. After that it had to be de husked. No mechanical tools for any of this work, it was all done manually by two young girls pounding the rice with a dheki. To keep the rhythm going they sang rhymes'

Midday the men went down to the river for their daily bath. After that the women and children would go. The children were washed first, then sent back home with an older sibling. Mum would wash the clothes and take her own bath. The washing would be festooned on bushes, it soon dried. When it was dried it was very carefully folded and placed under the mattress of the beds. No ironing necessary.
Clean clothes were taken from under the mattress ready smoothed and

fit to wear. Each evening the village men would meet under the Huge Banyan tree at the centre of the village and chat while having a quiet smoke.

When we had to get ready to go home, little gifts came from most of the families of the village and also some food carefully wrapped for our journey. When we finally got on the boat for the river crossing the whole village came to say good bye to us. I had been the first English Lady to have ever visited them. Sadly it was the last time, as the river was eroding the earth and the next rainy season the village fell into the river. As the villagers could see it was about to happen they dismantled all the buildings and took them much further in land quite a long way from the River to be safe. The village kept its same name but now it was a good mile from the River bank.

Water transport on the River. Padma (Ganges)

Left. Typical village house.

Chapter Ten

We were now flying high, our business was going very well, and each new Contract was being completed on time, we had a happy work force, and things were good. The office took up two ground floor rooms of the new wing of the house. The rest of the ground floor of the main house was an outside sitting room where I would see the tenant farmers who came from time to time, and discuss the crops, as my father-in-law got older he encouraged me to have an interest in the farms. Other rooms on the ground floor were guest rooms, as we always had relatives coming from Bagerhat or Pabna District. Also one guest suite with dressing room and Bathroom, this was used when my mother visited. We had a wide staircase leading from the hall; this staircase went right through the centre of the house up to the sun room on the roof. The first floor was divided up with a self contained one bed roomed apartment for my father-in-law, a manservant always slept in his apartment. A large dining hall leading in to a sitting room was on the right at the top of the staircase. Then to the left hand side of the staircase was our private apartment. This was six rooms, four bedrooms each with a dressing area, a family bathroom, another sitting room, and a small room I used for my sewing and craft, the children called it 'mammy's office'. This part of the house was air conditioned.

A large veranda overlooked the pond. The veranda was a lovely place to sit in the early morning and have that first cup of tea before the bustle of the day. I used to try to get up at dawn to see the beautiful sunrise come up over the tall coconut and beetle nut trees. The kingfisher would

be out early; it was a time of calm. I would sit on the veranda and the early morning sounds would gently increase as the house came alive. The sun would peep over the horizon promising another sunny day, I got used to it. When my mother visited she would say the same thing to me each day, 'look the sun is shining' she could never understand why we laughed. She would stay for about a month, when she was ready to make the long journey back to England she would say 'It hasn't rained once during my stay' she always visited in December and January, when the weather in Bangladesh is like a very good summer in England. Nights are cool enough to have a light quilt
on the bed. No need for the Air conditioning in the day time, as we had wall to wall sunshine all day. Within the surrounding wall we had lots of space not only for extending the main house if we wished, we also had another smaller building which was the main kitchen. As the ovens for the big kitchen were fuelled by wood, it could be very smoky, so this cook house was situated far enough away from us, in the main house. I did have a Kitchenette adjoining the dining room for my own use. Servants quarters were in the same area as the Cook house. The pond was well stocked with fish, Duncan and Nan, our very good friends would often come over in the afternoons to fish. The favourite catch was Tilapia. We would have it cooked in Oil with some onion and salt and pepper, cook would also make some chips, it was always delicious. Not having children of their own at that time, Nan was a very special 'Aunty' to my son. Everyone in my household called her 'Aunty Nan' also the children who lived in the family quarters at the Shipyard. Nan made soft toys as a hobby and gave them to the children, making sure every child had one. It was a sad day when they decided to go back to live in Scotland. Duncan had lived abroad for a long time and as they wanted to start a family, Duncan did not renew his contract.

    Before they left they planted some coconuts in their garden in the Shipyard. I always had coconuts if you keep them in an upright position the new tree sprouts out. Planting the whole nut completely in the ground with just the sprout sticking out, within five years that tree will bear coconuts. When ever I visited the Shipyard to see friends I always looked over to where they had lived to see how the trees were progressing.

Typical Khulna Street scenes.

Left, fast food Stall.

Below, New style buildings.

Chapter Eleven

The house in Khulna was in a nice residential area, the road was well made quite wide enough for traffic to pass easily. My son was about three years old when quite a strange thing happened. He had got to that very inquisitive stage where he had to look under every thing in the garden and he never seemed to be without a stick. Marching with his stick was a wonderful pass time and we would let him parade in the courtyard while we watched from a distance sitting on the veranda maybe with a nice cup of tea or a cool drink. It was on such a day when my son ran back up to the veranda, his face was full of excitement, he told me that there was a Tiger at the gate. I explained to him that, no! Tigers don't wander around in the town, we had very recently been looking at a picture book with a lovely picture of a Royal Bengal Tiger, and I had told him that the tigers lived in the Sundarbans, which was the rain forest about thirty miles away from Khulna.

Royal Bengal Tiger

I was convinced that he was imagining things. 'No, no Mammy, you have to come and see' he pulled on my arm, so I want with him to the gate. This was a gate of iron trellis which was only opened fully when a car needed to come into the courtyard, it was otherwise kept locked, mainly for safety. The gate did have a smaller latched gate for people to come through one at a time. As we approached I could see both of the gates were closed, the big gate was also locked as it should be. I asked him ' where is your tiger? He pointed through the gate. Of course there wasn't a tiger. 'Truly Mammy I did see the tiger'. To calm him down I said 'lets go and ask your Grandma about this', she would know how to take his mind off the tiger. My mother-in-law came back with us to the gate and we had a good look through, all the way up to the road. It had been raining that morning and there was a small patch of mud just on the other side of the gate. In the mud there was a huge paw mark. Could this be a tigers foot print? We decided that it must be some ones very large dog and moved back into the courtyard. Later that day my mother-in-law was telling my father-in-law about it all. He told us not to be silly.

Three days later news filtered through to us that a tiger had been loose in the Town, and as the Municipality did not wish for the population to panic, they kept it quite, and it was only after they had recaptured it, and taken it back to the zoo, they let it be known. So my son had seen the tiger.

The garden was quite large and I thought it was sensible to teach my children about the different things they may come across in the vegetation. One thing to warn them about was snakes. Pythons and Cobra's were among the different types of snakes to be found in Bangladesh. After explaining about snakes, off they would go to try to see a snake, every earth worm had to be inspected, 'is this a snake? They would ask and be very down in the mouth, when we told them it was only a lowly worm. As we had a large pond on our property the children before they could walk learnt to swim. I started taking them into the water at about nine months old. Ma did not like this, but as it was a hazard, I felt being able to swim was necessary. Ma would cover her eyes every time, when I first took one of them in, but when she saw that they could swim she would relax. All my children could swim before they could crawl. As Swimming aids,(such as water wings) were not available, I had looked around to see if I could find a substitute. Trying quite a few things that did not work out, or not practical, I finally tied two very dry coconuts together. This was done by pulling about an inch wide strand of the husk down about six inches and then tying the two coconuts together. They were very buoyant and the baby could float with the coconuts and learn how to swim. As my son got older he would bring his friends home with him from school. They all wanted to learn to dive and also learn the different swimming strokes. In Bangladesh they only seemed to do the 'dogpaddle' I had fun teaching them. After these 'lessons' the boys would all come in and have cake and a soft drink before going home. The favourite was always Ginger Parkin. Before it was all finished, I would have to hide a piece for my husband.

Solomon Age 14 years
Mary age 11 years
Monica Age 6 years

Chapter Twelve

I was settled in Khulna, the house was large but with a little bit of reorganization of the different rooms and there uses from when we first arrived, I had made it very comfortable. Living mostly on the first floor had an advantage, if there was any breeze it would come in off the veranda into the rooms. I could also see who was coming and going and watch the children. The cows and goats could be seen from this advantage point.

When Mary was two years old Ma went on a pilgrimage to Mecca. At that time mostly men went on the Pilgrimage, but my father-in-law wanted her to go with him, so they joined a local group of Pilgrims, and went by boat from Chittagong to Jeddah. While they were there they performed the Hajj. They were away two months. I missed Ma very much but it was also a busy time for me. My father-in-law left me in charge of all his enterprises in Khulna.

After retirement he had bought land and built low cost housing which he rented out, He had an agent who collected the rents, also he had a fleet of cycle Rickshaws which were hired out each day.

The rickshaws when returned at night sometimes needed some repair, at the rickshaw garage the mechanics worked hard to get these rickshaws road worthy for the next days hire. The head mistry would also take the money. Then bring it to me.

For some months before leaving for Saudi Arabia my Father-in-law had been showing me how it all worked, so that I would be able to look after his local businesses. We had agents and supervisors to do all this work but he left me on charge. He knew that I could understand what was happening and also who to contact if anything was needed. When he returned he was satisfied I had done the job well.

The following year during the month of Ramadan, Ma had not been feeling very well, she consulted our Doctor, she had high Blood pressure and against the Doctors orders she continued her Fast for one month. We later found she had a liver complaint, nothing could be done, we kept her at home and with the help of other ladies in the family we nursed her till her death.

She had been a second mother to me, she had taught me well. My father-in-law took it very hard. With the experience I gained when they went to Saudi Arabia; I was able to help him when he did not feel he wanted to see anyone.

The Farmers still came each season to talk to us about the crops, they were all Hindu and when they came the first time to see me, I invited them into my sitting room. On entering they gave me a Salam, by touching my feet, I did not like this practice and found it very embarrassing. When asked to sit down they wouldn't sit on the chairs indicated, the farmers apologised but said they were unable to sit on the chairs, thinking it may have something to do with their religion, I had the first meeting with them squatting on the floor.

This really was an impossible situation and as I would now be looking after the farms I needed to find a solution.

The Agent told me that they couldn't sit on the chairs because the Farmers heads would be above mine. At five foot nothing everybody's head is always above mine, so what was I to do?

One of the Farmers was at least six foot tall, with the nick name 'lombu' which in Bengali is very long or tall.

We employed a carpenter his name was Mannan, I got Mannan to make me some stools with short legs, these we found were low enough, and on testing with me sitting on my chair even 'lombu's' head would be lower than mine.

It was during one of these sessions with the farmers I said I liked goats, the next time they came to see me, they brought me a nanny goat. This started my heard off, as she was already having kids, and she always had them in threes. We soon had quite a few goats, the nanny would go to the farm and each time be covered by a different ram to keep my heard healthy, learning to milk them was interesting, it became one of my pleasures.

The farms kept me supplied with hay and straw for the cows, the children had the milk from the cows, from the Goats we could make a kind of Cheese.

My fathers family, the Smith's came from a very small village called Skipwith in North Yorkshire.. Grandad worked on the Forbes-Adams Estate and lived in a tied Cottage. Every Sunday the Family would go to Grandma's, this was where Aunts, Uncles and cousins would get together. Summer holidays Grandma always had some of us Grandchildren to stay, she had had twelve children, and none of the grandchildren were ever a bother to her. We would just tag along with Grandma, if she was picking berries on the common or going to her WI meeting we went too. Looking for eggs had been my job, climbing up into the hay stack and finding an egg to add to my basket was always very pleasing.

Remembering my childhood, when the hay came from the Farm I decided I was going to make a haystack. When it was finished the children loved it, we had a small bamboo ladder to enable us to climb up, soon the children's friends were coming over to sit in our haystack. As it was situated near enough to the Mango tree they could sit up there for hours, and still be in the shade.

Memories of home in Yorkshire

Chapter Thirteen

As we were so close to the Benapole Border and Calcutta on the other side in India, Calcutta was our nearest large City, with good shopping. So from time to time we would go for two or three days mixing sightseeing and shopping. We visited the zoo on one of these occasions, the children and I had quite recently seen the film Swiss Family Robinson and my daughter Mary had fallen in love with the Baby elephant, she was so delighted to see a baby elephant at the Calcutta zoo. After admiring him at some length we all moved on, but Mary must have sneaked back and when we realised she was no longer with our party we panicked. Children can so easily be stolen and money is demanded for their return, so while I stayed with the others my husband rushed back to where Mary had last been seen. Yes she had gone back to the baby elephant and, as in the film was saying 'come on baby elephant' like the little girl. After that we did try to keep a better control but she would get mesmerized and later that day we lost her in the main shopping Centre. Again we found her, she was watching some street puppets dancing After that her father took her hand and she had to walk with him, no escaping from his firm grip

When we went on our shopping trips we went by road on the Asian Highway. This was a concrete road that had not been well maintained, and although the trip was about seventy miles from Khulna it was a long rough journey. On the way we were fine, until just as we started to get into heavy traffic on the outskirts of Calcutta the horn of our can stopped working. If you have ever travelled in India or Pakistan you know it is most important to have a horn. Not only traffic on the road but it seems all humanity are wending along and encroaching onto the road, some pushing home made carts others with large bundles on their heads. Vendors with everything from live chickens and milk, vegetables and eggs. Hawkers with bundles of saris, others selling pots and pans, and the Holy cows that have right of way above anything else, wandering at leisure on the road, and people. Into this situation how could we drive without a working horn? My husband was driving and instead of asking the children to be quiet he ordered every one in the car to be the human horn, so on his command we all had to ' Beep Beep' at the top of our voices. We did get some funny looks, but they did give way, our loud 'Beep, beep's' worked and we got through and to our hotel with out any nasty incidents. The car went into the Garage and got a new horn, the only ones available at that time were for the Morris Oxford, so on our return journey when we sounded our horn, we sounded like the Calcutta taxis.

Right, a Calcutta Taxi and below a typical Calcutta Street.

Chapter Fourteen

Louder and louder the chanting could be heard, I must check that the children are safe, had they all returned from school? If not I must send a guard to escort them home. Now the slogans could be heard more clearly.

Political unrest with almost daily demonstrations and strikes were normal in the days of the early seventies.

When the British government gave freedom to the Indian sub-Continent in 1947, they decided to make a partition for the Muslims, this resulted in the creation of West Pakistan and East Pakistan, a thousand miles apart, on either side of India.

East Pakistan was really Bengal, and the people were Sunni Muslim, Christians and Hindu's.

On Independence, East Pakistan immediately became a satellite state of West Pakistan. Now twenty three years later Bengali's wanted their Country back. The English translation of Bangladesh is Bengali Land.

The Election had been held and the Bengali leader Sheikh Mozirbur Rahman had been elected by the people of East Pakistan, this did not suit the West Pakistan Government they would not accept the results. Sheikh Mozibur was a very popular leader and had the complete backing of the Bengali's having gained the majority of the votes in East Pakistan. Students were now leading the revolt.

What I could hear was another Political Demonstration; it was safer to stay at home out of the way.

Now the Army were clamping down on Students and known political figures. Arresting them and jailing without trial. Prominent people just disappeared, then some time later we would see in the Government controlled Newspaper, that they had been charged with many serious offences.

Students still kept up the momentum of Demonstrations and Strikes, disrupting Law and Order.

My husband said he needed to go to Dacca on business and although we knew it could be dangerous, and I begged him to stay at home until we could see what restrictions would be put on us, as Government Contractors, he still insisted on going.

I was at home with the children; my father-in-law now had the beginnings of Dementia so I was left in charge once again.

My husband had only been gone a couple of days when things started to turn really nasty, I listened to my radio, so I had some idea that all was not well, I prayed that my husband would return soon. I felt the further away from Dacca the better. Every thing seemed to be focused on the Capital of East Pakistan.

That night in March disaster struck. The Army surrounded the Halls of Residents of Dacca University and set fire to the buildings, as the students started to escape, they were shot. Some did get away and others had thankfully been staying in other places.

These students with help, left Dacca and disappeared into the village areas to form the Mukthi Bahini, (the freedom fighters) this was the start of the Civil war.

Left; Young men Training to be Freedom Fighters Right; Shiek Mozibur Rahman 'Civil War Breaks out'

We waited to hear from my husband, but for four days nothing Word had come through to Khulna about the Army burning the Students in their beds. The phones were down and we had no way of communication, to send someone to Dacca to look for him was not possible as the whole of Dacca seemed to be in chaos.

Some of the British people in Khulna were organising themselves and preparing to go to Dacca and then fly out of the Country.

I listened to the BBC world service, the announcer said anyone outside Dacca should stay where they were as it was too dangerous to travel.

The Army was searching Ferries and most River Launches for the fleeing Students. When they stopped the vessels they would search out the single young men and shoot them.

All the foreigners in Khulna left, I never heard from any of them again, I don't know if they reached safety or not. I was the only English person left in Khulna District.

I could speak fluent Bengali, now always dressed in a sari, my hair was long which I started to oil to make it look darker, also having dark brown eyes I could pass as a Bengali, I understood the culture, all around me I had family and a reliable work force, I felt quite safe. This would be, as long as I did not leave our house. To go out was very dangerous. If the Army should come into our house I hoped that being a mature lady with three children that the Army would not take me away, as we had heard about girls and young women being taken away.

The army rounded up all possible opposition.

Now that we were under fifteen hour curfew my men could not work, most of them now felt that they should try to get to their families in the rural areas where they would be safer, this was not so, as the Civil War progressed the Army with the help of the Police attacked villages where they thought the Freedom Fighters could be hiding.

So one little group after another said farewell to me, and went to their village homes. Our business came to a halt.

On the fifth day my husband returned, he had used what ever transport he could find, on the way he had been in a bazaar when the Police and the Army attacked the public, he was splattered with blood. To escape the massacre he had walked through pools of blood, his boots were in a terrible state. He had not washed for five days so he looked quite grey, which was from the dusty roads. Finding very little to eat or drink on this journey of over two hundred miles, he had lost a lot of his body weight and was dehydrated.

Later he told us how at dead of night, some one he knew came to his hotel and told him to get out of Dacca immediately. He left every thing there in the hotel; just taking his wallet and watch he disappeared into the night.

Walking to the edge of the City he could see the Halls of Residence burning, his old college was on fire, he first joined up with some students who had escaped, as soon as dawn came they decided to lie low and took refuge in a hut. Nearby villagers gave them water to drink and advice on which direction to go, so cross country they tramped, dodging road blocks and the Army patrolling the main Highway. Slowly they made their way, hopefully towards safety, mostly by night, one by one each person dropping off the group, going in the direction of their village, finally my husband was now alone he found his way to the river which he would have to cross. He hailed a country boat and offering them money, and asked to be taken to the other bank. After getting into the boat he realised he was on a river Pirate's boat and they had just plundered another craft. Blood stained weapons were with their loot in the bottom of the Boat. When they set him down on the other side of the river. He gave them the money they had agreed on and also in good will he also gave them his Omega Sea master watch.

Many people were now on the road and so along he tramped, he had lost his suit jacket some where, and also his money had run out. He had a ring which he always wore on his small finger, this was a family heirloom, he used the ring to barter for some food. This is how he got back to Khulna.

After recovering from his journey he considered our position. Should we stay in our own home in Khulna or should we try to find a safer place for myself and the children. Maybe somewhere in one of our Village homes.

My father-in-law was very much against the children and I going anywhere, but finally my husband decided that we should go to Bagerhat on the other side of our river, the village home of my mother-in-law would be the safest place for us.

We couldn't take a lot with us and we had to be ready to walk must of the way. My son and Mary were old enough to walk some way but Monica was not walking yet so we would have to carry her.

The next time Curfew was lifted we left our home behind, me and the three children with my husband leading the way. For safety I wore a full Burkha which had belonged to my Mother-in-law. I don't know why we had kept it, most Burkha's are black but Ma's was a deep purple, it didn't have a nylon veil like most Burkha's but one that was hand crocheted. Not a fashion item.

Crossing the river in a small ferry boat passed without incident, it had recently rained, the Monsoon was just beginning, the roads on the other side of the river were mud roads, hardened by the hot sun, but as soon as the rains came, turned into deep rutted muddy roads. Rickshaws had difficulty getting along and as there were many travellers, there was not enough rickshaws for everyone. We decided to walk some way; maybe we would get some transport further along the road.

We had been walking since early afternoon, the children were very subdued and when it was my turn to carry Monica I thought she felt very hot, did she have a temperature? We were not used to travelling like this and now beginning to feel tired.

As we passed by a small hamlet a little girl called Rhokia recognised my daughter Mary, they both went to the same school, she ran inside her hut and told her mother. When her mother came to see who was passing she recognised my son too. After speaking to them she came towards me and said 'Begum Sahiba, you must come inside and take some rest'. I accepted and went into her hut. She sent her brother to catch up with my husband and ask him to join us.

Rhokia's mother like us had left her home in Khulna for the safety of her village home. On hearing where we were heading to, she asked us to stay the night and she would try to find out if it was in fact safe for us, to go to Bagerhat.

Refugees Fleeing from their homes.

The small wooden bed she had available was large enough for us to sit on together. With Monica lying across my knee all night we sat and waited for the morning. Monica had a high temperature by now, and the news was not good from Bagerhat. I had had enough I wanted to go back to my own house in Khulna, my attitude was 'if we die, lets die in our own home'

We went back to Khulna, we had to wait at the side of the river for Curfew to be lifted in Khulna, then we crossed again on the small river boat, my father-in-law had something to say to his son, but he was very happy to have us back. We now had to look at our security and safety.

Chapter fifteen

When the Pakistani Army attacked the students in their beds, panic was created among the population and instead of the Army gaining the upper hand, the resistance movement rather than being squashed gained momentum.

Feeling safer in the rural area's families went to their village homes, others felt that they would be safer crossing the border into India.

All along the Border just inside India transit Camps were set up for the Bengali Refugees. Those lucky enough to have friends or family living in India soon fled. Many Offices were closed due to the Curfew imposed and also the dwindling of staff. Life in the towns and city's was survival, don't go onto the roads during Curfew, anyone found doing so were shot. Also try not to come to the attention of the Army, and look to your own safety and safety of those who were with you. Markets would spring up suddenly as soon as Curfew was lifted and every one would try to get something to eat. Choice did not come into it, if it was for sale it was bought and taken home cooked and eaten.

Soon there were shortages of everything. Nothing was coming into the Towns from the villages, fresh vegetables, chickens and eggs soon disappeared from the Market. Fishermen were not going out to fish and the Abattoir was closed.

Life was getting hard for every one. Having money did not help when there is nothing to buy. We had a small general store which had been built in to the Boundary wall of our home. We had a Manager to run it for us, it was always well stocked with basic items of food,

Cigarettes tobacco and sweets and bottled soft drinks, apart from being the local shop, laundry could be left for the dhobi Walla.

Before my husband returned from Dacca, the manager and his family had decided to go to their village so the shop was shut. Fearing that it might be ransacked I ordered all the goods to be brought in to the house, we did not know then that the Civil War would last for nine months but it was certainly a good move.

Just after my husbands return and we understood how dangerous life would become, some of our close relatives came to live in our house, this we allowed as we felt there would be safety in numbers.

Before when anyone came to our home, there was never a question of not being hospitable, but under these circumstances we felt we needed to have some rules regarding their stay. Firstly where were all these people going to live in the house? We had some large storage sheds which were used for storing equipment for our Engineering work. As this equipment was at our different work sites there was plenty of spare room to store furniture and spare domestic items and carpets. No shortage of man power we started to strip the house of all things not essential to make more room for our extended family. We then divided the house up with one family unit in each room. Cramped to say the least but as we were all family we would make it work.

Now everyone had somewhere to sleep we had to think of cooking. My servants had now gone so I felt that each family unit should cook for themselves. We made some earthen cooking ovens, one for each family unit, each cooking oven was in a small thatched roofed shelter. As it was March and the dry season this was OK for the time being, some shelter could be had from the sun while cooking. Each family unit would cook and feed themselves. We had rice and dhal, fish in the pond and vegetables in the garden. We were quite self contained inside our walled property.

At first we felt that we were on a picnic, but as time went on cracks did appear in most relationships, due to the fear and extreme pressure we were all under.

I became the smoker's best friend, I had cigarettes, we didn't smoke ourselves. I knew who was a smoker so they could have one cigarette a day. The ingenuity of trying to get more. Wives who came and told me a sob story or two, non-smokers who suddenly claimed to be secret smokers, they tried everything. I stuck to my guns and as the stock dwindled and the war went on they thanked me for not giving in, in those early days.

We also had sweets, so the children also got a ration each day, I must say the children were quite happy about the arrangement and I never had any problem with them. The other items from the shop, they could have at cost price. When all this was over we would have to stock the shop again. When it was gone it was gone so everyone economised and wastage was down to nil.

Rice is sold in the bazaar, so if they needed rice as soon as the Curfew was lifted the men would go to see what they could find in the bazaar. In emergency we did have a rice store inside our house. With the well stocked pond and as there was no work to go to, the men and boys would go and do a spot of fishing, it helped to pass the time. We had lots of coconut trees and beetle nut trees, so the more agile of the men would climb the trees for these.

Soon the mango trees would have ripe fruit and the banana plants all had crops growing. The vegetables and green chillies were growing in the garden, everyone could have what they needed.

We had some time back sunk a deep well for our own drinking water. The Municipality drinking water was a good half a mile away. When our neighbours had such a short time to go to the bazaar and collect enough water for their families they had a problem. We had a side gate into our property and we let it be known that they could take drinking water from our well.

I had two cows and some goats so as long as they had milk then the younger children could have that.

One day when the curfew had been lifted I heard a vendor going down the road, calling 'eggs, eggs for sale'. I called him into the courtyard and after some haggling purchased all the eggs from him. What joy, we had boiled eggs. fried eggs. omelettes and best of all an egg korma curry. Delicious.

Before this we had got down to Boiled rice, Dhal. fried vegetables with green chillies and fish from the pond which was mostly Tilapia Fish, however nice this food is it had started to get boring.

About this time we started to have little parties for the children in the afternoons. We made some snacks and we had sweets, games and competitions were organised, this was to try to help the children cope with the situation we were all in. Children do worry, and with the adults always being so tense we had these little parties about twice a week. Children would come from our neighbour's houses too, even if the Curfew was in force.

We had all learnt to climb the high walls which surrounded our homes, going onto the road was mostly avoided, this practice of wall climbing could be useful if we needed an escape route.

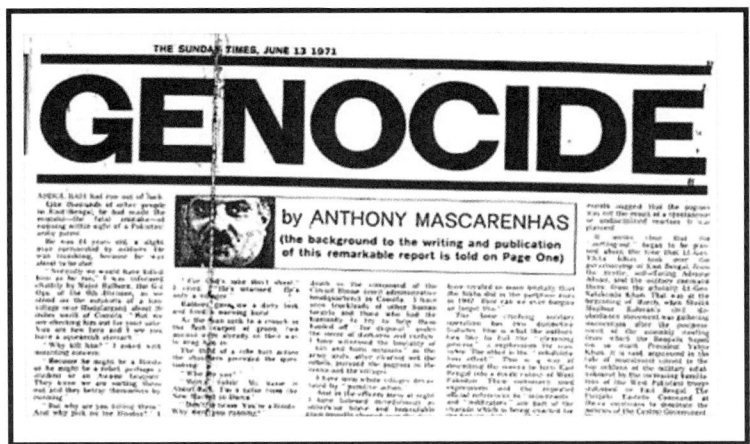

The Sunday Times -June 13th 1971

Each time the men went to the Bazaar they would come back with dreadful stories about what was happening to people. We did not have any news papers and we did not know if the Foreign Press knew about the Genocide which was going on in our Country. Many times we would say among our selves where is the UN are they not going to help us? Still the Army continued with chastising the Bengali's

I heard about the Army going to the Girls High School and also the Ladies College and selecting girls and taking them away, these Girls were kept in Brothels for the soldiers.

The ladies inside my house tried to stay out of sight after hearing about these poor girls. Still Army Officers would call and expect to be given tea.

Chapter Sixteen

We were basically happy to be together and wished that the Civil war would be over soon. We tried not to think of the danger we were all in. No school for the children, at first they were happy about this But they soon got bored. As the school year starts in January, and we were in April by now, we would teach the children at home, so that when they went back to school, they would not have lost a year. In Bengali schools you have to pass your Exams yearly, this enables you to go into the next year, if you don't pass you have to stay in the same year.

As our son, Solomon was at The Catholic School for Boys and my daughter Mary at the Coronation School for Girls they had to keep up with their studies. We also had baby Monica. Also on the safety front a rota was made for night duty. As the Army had a nasty trick of trying to get the men onto the road during Curfew, sometimes even starting fires or setting fire to empty buildings, we had to be vigilant at night.

In the early days the Army's tactics worked and if men went onto the road in Curfew the Army would line them up against the walls and shoot them for breaking the Curfew. Rows of dead bodies against the boundary walls were there in the morning for everyone to see.

After dark the first watch would begin. Four hours duty on the roof, watching, and being ready for action if necessary. Then the next watch would take over and so on through the night.
Silence had to be maintained as the Army did not like to be seen doing these things. As we were prepared, we stayed safe. Not so some of our neighbours. One night the army tried to take one of our next door

neighbours, but the ladies in the house made such a noise and alerted the neighbourhood, that the Army went away only after I saw them about to cut our neighbours throat with a bayonet.

Our road was mostly residences of Business men, Doctors Lawyers, and College Professors with the exception of one Hindu Gentleman who was a well known Classical Singer and was also my daughter Mary's Music Teacher.

One night the Army came and burnt the Hindus house which was diagonally opposite ours. It was truly dreadful, we knew the family had thankfully gone to India and the house was empty but a lot of very valuable musical instruments were destroyed in the fire. To try to keep the children quite while this was happening so close, was the job of the mothers. This was not just my own children but others who were living in our house. Sometimes there was nothing for it, but to put our hands over their mouths.

In the day time the Army would just arrive and want to search a house, they were looking for weapons or any young men who could possible belong to the Mukthi Bahini. At this time some young men did stay in my house under the guise of being a servant. They were students who had joined the Mukti Bahini and after some fierce fighting stayed for two or three days rest before going and joining the fighting again. I did not know their real names or where their families lived it was safer that way. Also the army were looking for good quality broad band radios.

Listening to the radio was banned and also playing of patriotic music. I had a radio which my father-in-law brought back for me from Saudi Arabia when he went to perform Hajj. We had to find somewhere to hide it.

Going up to the roof there was a small store room where we kept spare Deck chairs. It had a door and was very private, no light but very out of the way. With my husbands engineering skills we installed the radio in this small room. I was able to go each day (at our time three o'clock) to listen to BBC World Services nine o'clock news. First the call signal of Oranges and Lemons then the English voice saying 'This is London'. I also listened to other News services and then I would report to the household what, if anything, was happening in Bangladesh and the outside World. Only my husband and I knew the true location of the Radio, not even the children who could innocently tell the wrong people. I had no contact with England for nine months.

The door of one of our ground Floor store rooms was left unlocked at night. Every evening I would leave cooked rice and some Curry, fried vegetables and Dhal, they were covered over with plates, and also a large pot of drinking water and some mugs. Bedrolls would be stacked against the wall. In the morning I would go down and clear everything away, and if the bed rolls had not been stored near the wall I generally tidied up so that there was not any evidence of anyone having been there. Dirty rags which they had cleaned their weapons with I burnt.

On each visit I made sure that the children did not see me enter this store room, during the day the Storeroom was always locked and I had the key. We were giving sanctuary to the Mukti Bahini, they came on the understanding that they came after dark, made no noise and were gone before dawn. Only my husband and I knew about this arrangement. No one living in our house even knew about these gallant young men staying the night.

We had a large pond and at it furthest point away from the house and other buildings it almost met the boundary wall. Here wrapped in plastic bags guns and ammunition were stored. The Freedom fighters could collect what they needed and they would be unobserved as this area was where goats grazed under the coconut trees where the vegetation was lush.

There was cruelty and famine for the village people

Chapter Seventeen

I heard the screech of the jeeps tyres. They had stopped outside our house. Although it was day time Full Curfew was in force.
What did the Army want with me?
I was frightened, the Civil war had been going on now for a few months and I had become involved. I was still wearing a golden locket on a chain around my neck. On this locket was the Election symbol of Shiekh Mozibur Rahman, which was a country boat, with this symbol I was identified by the young freedom fighters if they should need to stay longer than just the night in our house. They could speak to me with confidence. Had someone betrayed me to the Army?

At the same time quite a few of the young Army officers visited our home, asking if they could do a spot of fishing in their off duty time. Really it was in hope of catching a glimpse of my very pretty eldest daughter. But I had to be welcoming and act friendly towards them, I kept an eye on them in case they should approach a danger zone. Allowing them to fish and have tea, could put us above suspicion and be insurance for our safety.

There was a jeep with a machine gun mounted on the front and also one on the back. I had been told that my dogs would give chase to the Army jeeps and secretly the dogs had the nick name of 'Mukti Bahini'. Anyone wearing a lungi was OK with them and they didn't give chase or bark but they did not like army uniforms. What had happened was my guard dog had had a litter, normally we would send the puppies, when they were big enough to our different farms in the villages. This time because of the unrest we were not able to do this. So the puppies had stayed with their mother. We now had quite a few dogs. They were all good guard dogs and always gave warning of anyone entering our property. Were the Army going to give me a warning regarding the dogs chasing their jeep?

The Officer came into the house asking for me. Without telling my husband why, they put me into the jeep and took me away. I asked the young officer 'where are we going', I said it very gently, and he told me 'to the Maternity hospital, Memsahib, I have had orders to take you there'. This was quite mystifying to me. I had nothing to do with the Maternity Hospital and I certainly was not having a baby. It wasn't a long journey, in fact I could have got there in ten minutes on foot. I was dropped off and the jeep went away. A nurse came out onto the veranda and said 'We are glad to see you'. I couldn't see why as I was not medically trained, what was the problem? Quite often people would ask me for help, thinking that being a white lady I would be able to do something for them. Sometimes I helped with Hospital admission as money had to be exchanged before even the most urgent cases were admitted, or with the purchase of Medicines which could be very expensive.

In the maternity hospital they had a patient in labour with her first baby, she had been in labour too long and mother and baby were getting tired, plus the baby was rather large for the slim young mother. I asked them 'why do you need me?. 'You're an English Lady and you help people'. They told me that in this situation the patient should be transferred to the District hospital, but they couldn't do this as we were under Curfew. Ambulances were only allowed for Army personnel during Curfew. 'We haven't got a Doctor in the hospital, just the one midwife and two nurses, we know you can help deliver this baby'

Being English and knowing Bengali was my qualification to deliver the child. So they had asked the Army to bring me. No training, but I had helped out at some births. This had been done under Curfew conditions by climbing over walls going from one property to another to help a mother giving birth. Somehow the nurses had heard about me helping . Now I had to deliver this baby with the help of the midwife and one nurse. The other nurse was still asleep as she had been on duty all night and not been able to get home.

Both of them were of the the opinion that the lady should have a Caesarean Section. The midwife soon had me in a gown and scrubbed up, First thing was to calm the mother down, she was in no state of mind to deliver this baby. Every thing seemed to be normal apart from this being a first baby. The young mother was known to me, she seemed to calm down and followed my instructions. We all decided that it was time for baby to say hello to the world. After about an hour we delivered her with a healthy baby boy. Mother and baby were asleep when the Curfew was lifted, I quickly made my way home to tell them all about it. I had things to attend to.

Every one was pleased to see me safe and sound. Still stories were rife about people being taken away and not seen again.

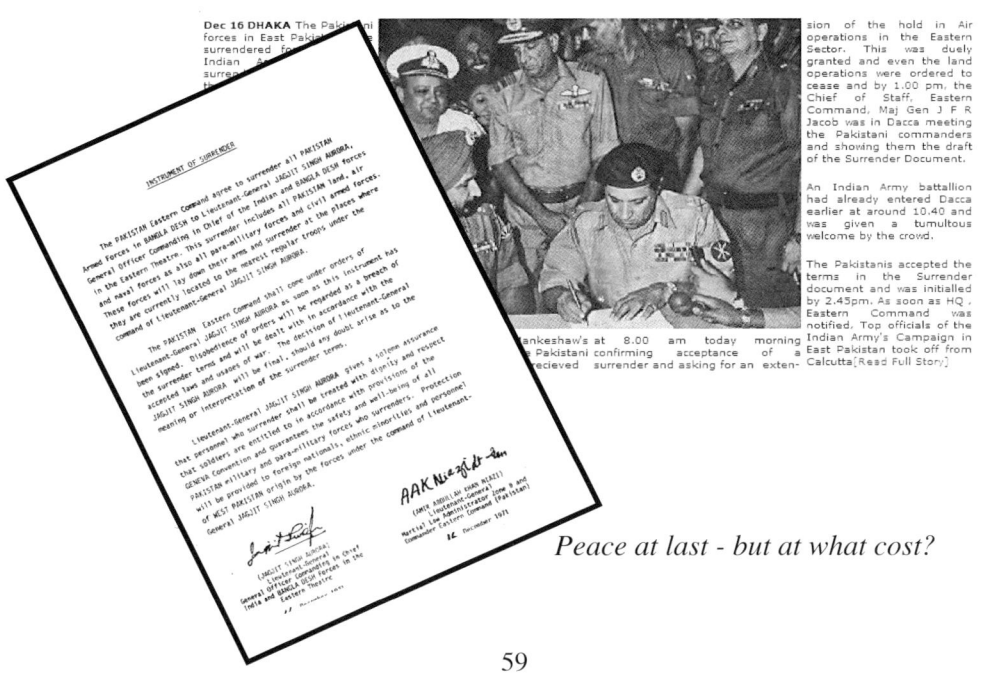

Peace at last - but at what cost?

Chapter Eighteen

Bangladesh was free, but at what price? Thousands of people lost their lives, and many Families were displaced, crops had not been planted, but, we were once again free. After the civil war had been going for nine months things were coming to a head.

The Army started to destroy the telephone exchange and the local radio station. Curfew was now 24 hours. We were all prisoners in our own homes. Then the bombing started. When my husband heard the bombs dropping, he went to the cook house and came back wearing a wok on his head, it was quite funny as the wok must have still had some type of gravy in it and, the wok had not been washed. Gravy was running down each side of has cheeks. He didn't seem to mind and was quite pleased with his 'good idea', plus the protection he thought he would have.

I took the children under the central staircase. We got some mattresses and cushions to make ourselves comfortable, every time a bomb came over we covered our ears with our hands. The whole building would shake, fortunately we did not have glass windows, the windows were metal grills with wooden shutters, after wards we found shrapnel scattered all over the courtyard. After the bombing stopped we sat there waiting to see what would happen next. We heard a rumbling sound in the distance and as it got nearer we realised a tank was coming up our road. Although we were frightened I tried to stay calm so that the children would not panic. We had got this far and I was beginning to have confidence that we were nearing the end of the Conflict. The tank stopped outside our house, and we heard voices. Someone was asking for me, by name in Hindi. The tank came into our courtyard, it was an Indian tank.

The Indian Army arrives.

The officer told us that they had liberated Khulna. He asked about my welfare and said if I could quickly write a letter to my parents he would take it and post it in Calcutta for me. When my Mam and Dad got the letter it was the first communication they had received from me for nine months. It seems I was the only foreigner left in Khulna District so when the Press correspondents came through our town they always called in at our house. The Bazaar was now open, but they had very limited goods to sell, also they were very expensive. By now we didn't have much cash left, although we had assets, cash was what we needed most.

I had a Standard Ensign Estate Car and within days of the Pakistan Surrender my driver came back to Khulna. It was easy to get a taxi licence, so every day my driver took the car to the taxi rank offering trips to the Benapole Border. People were moving in both directions across the Border so it was not difficult to get the return trip back to Khulna. The driver Hassan was Muslim and his helper Gore a Hindu, they made up a very good team. Each day after paying for petrol, and paying their wages I still had enough cash for my household expenses. As the workers returned we had to see what was left at our different sites. The machinery was of no use to anyone so, with a little maintenance it was soon ready for use again. The sites were opened and in good faith we started work again. The little cash we now had, we kept for the workers wages. Banks were still not open for business. We had a fleet of cycle rickshaws which we hired out daily, the hire charge was always paid in cash. Soon the shop manager returned and with the money from the cycle rickshaws I was able to restock the shop, so now we had the shop up and running. Things were beginning to get back to normal.

Our farmers were all Hindu, and were tenant farmers, in Bangladesh the system is, the owner of the farm and land, gets half of the produce. When the farmers and their families returned I was able to give them some rice and money for seed. But still we had to face Famine in Bangladesh. Foreign aid was coming into the country, this was a great help to the general population of Bangladesh.

We had a new flag. Originally it was to be a green flag with the shape of Bangladesh in Yellow in the centre. In fact my husband got me to make one but, to be mass manufactured it was too complicated and everyone wished to fly the national flag. In the end it was settled, the National Flag would be a Green flag with a Red Disc in the Middle. Around this time Save the Children rented a small one storied building on the corner of our road, they opened a clinic and feeding centre. I got to know the English nurses who came to the clinic each day and started to go down to help them with some translation. We got on so well that they offered me a job, I opted to stay as a volunteer.

A Family planning clinic was opened, I was able to talk to the ladies so I tried to educate the ladies regarding conception. Most ladies who already had some children, felt that by taking the pill, which we offered free, they could control the size of their family. One day I met one of these ladies and she was obviously pregnant, but I also knew she had been calling each month for her pill. I asked her about the pill and she said 'it doesn't work, I gave my husband a pill every night and still I got pregnant' In the class I had told them about the mans part in conception and she had mistakenly thought that he should take the pill. The husband and the baby were fit and healthy afterwards.

The Bengali calendar months, start in the middle of the English calendar months, and this led to some confusion in the Anti Natal Clinic which the English nurses ran. My father-in-law hearing of their difficulties made a chart of the Bengali months with the corresponding dates on English, the nurses found it a great help to them.

Many of the children who came to the clinic were malnourished, the nurses set up a feeding clinic and each morning the children registered for food would sit in long rows on the ground and they were given nourishing food to eat. Very quickly the children improved; as one group improved another group would come in for registration. A guard had to be posted at the door of the clinic to keep law and order. Save the Children do a wonderful job and their nurses give two years of their life to help others. Some even coming back for a second tour of duty.

From my upstairs sitting room I had a good view of my neighbour's property where they also had a pond. During this time I heard lots of shouting and lamenting I called over, to ask what the matter was. A little girl had fallen into their pond and although they had got her out, she must have been in the water for some time, they thought she was dead. I told them to run with her to the Clinic, I knew that Angela and Judy, the two English Nurses were still clearing up after the morning Clinic.

I also ran to the clinic meeting the casualty in the entrance at about the same time. Judy and Angela started to work on the little girl and managed to remove quite a lot of water from her lungs. Then she spluttered and came round. She was transferred to the District Hospital, she made a complete recovery.

I was often by myself due to the re-establishment of the business. My husband would be away visiting the different work sites, only coming home for a day or two for a change of clothes, and to attend his Rotary Club meetings. Running the house was left to me. I enjoyed the different activities I was involved with and always seemed to be busy. The Children were back at school and my neighbours had all returned, we were settling down but it was early days and we still had problems to face.

Chapter Nineteen

In Bangladesh there is a high percentage of people with Cataracts. Treatment is available but, only in the towns and cities and can be costly. In the village areas the poor who are affected by this go blind, some are looked after by their families, or hope for hand outs and wander the village with one hand on a young child's shoulder, in the other hand a stick. Ultimately they become beggars, sometimes coming to the towns but very few get treatment.

The Rotary Club of Khulna saw the need for an Eye Camp, where this simple operation could be performed and in most cases eyesight can be restored. A rotary Club in Canada were willing to send a medical team to us, so we got very busy organising the Eye Camp, this was to be our project for the year. One of our Rotary members Islam Bhai, had a cold storage unit in Khulna, this was empty in the cooler months of the year, and as this was the best time to hold the Camp we decided to accept his kind offer of the main cold storage building, and offices. As soon as the cold storage season was over, we set about transforming the building into a temporary hospital. The large space would be an open ward for after surgery patients, the Director's office would be the operating Room, and the main office the Consulting Rooms and Clinic.

Everything was made ready for the arrival of the two eye Surgeons and there assistants. We would provide the post-op Care under their guidance. About a week before the Doctors arrival men want out to the surrounding villages and told all the villages about the Eye Camp, The Doctors arrived and each taken to the family they would be staying with. Next day, still not sure how many patients would arrive we opened our doors for business. A large number came that first day; all were seen by the Doctor and assessed for operation. As always there were some we could not help, but the ones we could, were asked to stay for an operation next day. When we made the announcements in the villages we had told the patients that they needed to come with a bed roll and one family member, also to be prepared to stay with us for up to one week. The important thing was that there would be no charge, operations, food and medicines would be free. The lucky ones soon settled in, and bed rolls were quickly laid out in rows. At first the patients were very nervous but as they got to know their neighbours soon settled down. Some of them had never slept in a brick building before. The smells were different too, as we had used a lot of disinfectant when cleaning. It smelt like a hospital.

Day two the clinic opened to even more people, who came to be assessed, maybe it was the very brave ones who came on the first day, those who had not heard the men who went into the villages with the megaphones were told about us. All of the following week we had full clinics. The afternoon of day two we started the operations. A local anaesthetic was given and with surprising speed the discs of jelly which formed the cataract were whipped off. Bandages on and back to the main ward to rest. It was done two by two, and the patients waited in a queue to go in. Some of the ladies were very shy of the white men but we were there to help them and encourage them to be brave. Operations went on most of the afternoon, the Rotary members and their ladies worked on a rota, so we would stay until the evening meal was served We had opted to work in the Camp. We would take it in turns to do the medicine round and make sure everyone was comfortable before we went home. The Doctors after the last operation went to their host family for some well earned rest, only to start all over again the next day. The assistant with the team checked the patients and after a few days the bandages were ready to come off. The team had also brought with them hundreds of used glasses which if possible they would issue to the patients before going home. A dispensing optician was able to fit the correct lens in to the frames and most of our patients went home with smart new glasses.

The Medical team departed after a fortnight with us, in that time they had performed over twelve hundred operations and treated many others who were not suitable for operation, but had other eye complaints A local Optician and a Doctor took over with the after care, our eye camp had been a success. Rotary International Clubs were very popular in Bangladesh, we all helped each other and when the need arose, we asked for unwanted sewing machines, we had many donations. The Rotary ladies wanted to teach women how to sew for themselves and some of them if proficient to work along side the male tailors. At the end of each course we were able to give them a Certificate and also a sewing machine. Things had changed since the forming of Bangladesh and already even if you could afford to keep servants they were hard to find. I had always designed and sewn my children's clothes and also done Craft work, when we set up little sewing groups, twice a week young ladies were coming for tuition. Most of these ladies could crochet and in exchange for me teaching them to knit, they taught me to crochet. I love to crochet and design babies shawls, and buggy blankets, which I still do and sell, at the Country Market here in England. Lots of Aid organisations were coming into Bangladesh and gradually the country got back onto its feet, the people are so resilient, many suffered but they put it all behind them and worked hard for the country they love.

The rice is dried and turned in the sun, as it has always been.

Chapter Twenty

When the young men came back to their homes after being Freedom Fighters, it took some time for them to adjust to normal life again but, there were young teenage girls who had to try to adjust too. These young girls had been stolen by the army, violated and kept for the Comfort of the Soldiers. When they were taken they were young innocent teenage girls, some of very good families, not all the families welcomed them back, wrongly thinking that their families had been dishonoured.

The men were killed the girls were violated and cast aside

After some time the ladies of the Rotary club took an interest in these young girls and if they wanted to go back into education would go with the girl to see the Headmistress and help the girl to be readmitted into school.

As we were already holding our Craft Classes, if they were interested we included them into the classes. All these young ladies were of marriageable age but, in a country where the bride should be chaste this could be difficult. Some of the young freedom fighters, did offer marriage to these young girls but, the ladies in Rotary made sure that these Boys were able to take a wife. We made certain that these girls would not go into an unsuitable marriage only to suffer again. From our fund raising we had a special fund for some clothes for the Bride and Groom as is traditional, We asked the groom to give a gold ring at the time of betrothal. When the date was set we held the marriage ceremony and all of us contributed to the feast. If possible we tried to get the families involved and once the marriage took place some of the families felt more comfortable with what had happened to their daughters.

Chapter Twenty One

After the civil war in 1971 then came the Famine. Crops had not been sown and although the Civil War had only lasted for nine months we had missed two harvests. Everyone in Bangladesh eats Rice, some Aid had come from abroad, but not enough, so many were faced with starvation. My husband was a member of the Rotary Club also we had a lot of agricultural land which produced plenty of grain to feed us, and our extended family for more than a year, other years we would sell quite a bit to the rice dealers.

People were dying, every day I could see mothers or fathers carrying dead babies and young children for burial. Feeling something should be done I enquired from my husband, about Soup Kitchens and was shocked to find that the Municipality authorities were so afraid of a riot. They were doing nothing apart from policing the Ration shops.

When I asked my husband if we could do something to help he replied that it was too dangerous. My eldest daughter Mary was 10 years old and I told her how upset I was about the situation, we had so much, what could we do? I had some broken rice, which we gave to the chickens, could this be cooked into a type of porridge? How could we feed people? Mary and I decided that we would take the chance.
Remembering what my husband had said, I knew he would stop us, so Mary and I made a plan. We knew who we could trust to keep a secret.

People were dying of hunger we could feed a very limited number of people, so we decided that we would feed children. Mary would make contact with 10 children (who were always coming around the back entrance) asking for anything edible.

She would tell ten children that, if they came at midday she would find something for them, the condition would be that they kept it a secret and not tell anyone, if they did she would not give them any food. We had to limit numbers so that it would not be noticeable, then our Secret would be out.

In a large pot I got our cook to cook the gruel. What could we use for plates? The boy who looking after the cows was sent to cut some banana leaves,(these can be made into pokes to fill with the gruel). If he was seen doing this it would be thought that it was for the goats. No plates no evidence.

On the first day twelve o'clock arrived and we went to the back gate. Yes ten hungry children were quietly waiting to see if they would get anything. They had to eat on the spot and if they did not tell anyone, they could come again the next day and we may have something for them. They kept their side of the bargain and came each day and we gave them some gruel, also anything else we could find that would not be missed. Having a good supply of fruit and vegetables it was quite easy to find something. Until things improved we continued feeding 10 children each day, my husband never found out.

My husband sometimes had Rotary friends around to our house for committee meetings and it was at such a meeting, while serving tea, I mentioned how I felt that we should be doing something for the starving people.

Every evening the hungry would be outside the Court House and other Government Buildings in the centre of town, hoping that some one would give them some food, these people were not vagrants but dying of hunger.

Business men want to think, that they have thought up all good ideas, so I steered them to think of a way we would be able to help. I knew the Rotary ladies would be willing to help.

The men decided that if the ladies could manage to make some roti and spiced vegetables we could make wraps. At evening prayer time they could take their cars with the drivers, and slowly go past these hungry people, open the window of the cars enough to pass the wraps out, the driver always to be ready to drive off if any trouble should start. They were terrified of starting a Riot. The first evening the men went out with the wraps, we ladies waited hoping that the plan would work. The Rotarians wives had been busy, with the help of our cooks, preparing the wraps. The men were jubilant 'Their' plan had worked and this help was given each evening until things improved.

Solomon 13 years, Mary 10 years, Monica 5 years.

Chapter Twenty Two

The house was decorated with coloured electric lights and speakers were already fitted at each corner of the flat roof of the house, for the music. Yet again we were having a wedding at our house. Since the birth of Bangladesh weddings had been put on hold. Every one had financial difficulties and recovery was slow for many businesses. The famine had not been a suitable time to be celebrating with a feast, even if you had food and could afford the expense of a wedding. The girls were all getting older and as it was still the tradition for girls to be married by the time they reached their early twenty's parents were getting worried. The marriageable boys had all had their education disrupted so it was catch up time, now three years on we were having lots of weddings. Our house was the house of choice for our relatives as we had plenty of room. Many nieces were married in our house. As a wedding could be conducted in your own home with the Registrar coming with the priest from the Mosque, all that was needed was a Bride and Groom with two witnesses. Also some large buildings could be hired if you wanted a large wedding. Our house was large enough to host a medium sized wedding, we could accommodate family and about 200 guests could sit down to a meal. The upper floor of the house and the flat roof above was reserved for the Ladies, the roof which was decorated with a large marquee, with coloured electric lights all the way around, had trestle tables and chairs set out, this was where the ladies would eat the wedding feast. Gentlemen would be on the front lawn in another Marquee. Amplifiers being scattered around the house and grounds playing the latest hit songs. Trestle tables and benches were hired, Cooks and their assistant would arrive with their large cooking pots and set up an open air kitchen in the courtyard. Large earthen ovens were made about a week before hand for the huge cooking pots which the Biryani would be cooked in. When the couple have decided or agreed to get married things move very quickly, Most eastern people will consult an astrologer who will be able to tell the family which dates would be suitable for the match. This all depends on the phase of the Moon and the Birth signs of the bride and Groom. The date decided on, now is the time for the parents, aunts and uncles, of the Bride and Groom to get together and start making all the arrangements. This helps the two families to bond before the wedding, which is a good idea.

In Bangladesh the bride still gets a Dowry. Depending on the Brides family's wealth or lack of, but it will be a set of clothes for the Groom, sari's petticoats and blouse for the Bride and most fathers will try to give at least one piece of jewellery. If the brides family are wealthy, a lot of jewellery will have to be made for her. Some brides receive furniture from their father for their new home, but most young couples start married life in the boy's family home. The Groom gives a ring to his Bride at the time of confirming they will marry. This is a time for action, Brides mothers and aunties go into over drive, The jewellery design books are pored over, price of Gold discussed, different pieces chosen, then the Order is placed. At the same time the Brides father is deciding where to have the Wedding. Hiring the cooks who will come with his team of helpers, also at this time estimating how many people to invite. Family members don't usually get a formal invitation, they get to know all the details on the family grapevine and it is normal to just turn up. If they are coming any distance they will be given some accommodation. Official invitations are sent out asking for a RSVP, in this way you come to an estimated number. Once the cooks have an idea of numbers, plans are given to the host, shopping list given, quantities are worked out and the shopping begins. Most lists will include a cow or two goats and maybe a few chickens. The cow or goat is for the Biryani which it is traditional wedding food. Other items are for two or three days before the wedding. This shopping is done in relays with the girl's father overseeing every thing. This is the time for the ladies in the family to do some serious retail therapy. Cosmetics and fragrant oils are usually at the top of the list. Clothes for the whole Family, and for the household right down to the last servant, who must have a new set of clothes to wear on the wedding day. Weddings are celebrated over a few days. Day one is the Brides pamper day, all her girl friends and female relatives come ready to start preparing her for the big day .Bengali's are quite happy people and do love a good joke. This is a time of ladies only, so quite a lot of teasing goes on. The older ladies are there to tell stories of their own marriages and it all gets very intimate. Mendi leaves are collected and crushed into a paste, (now it is available in a tube, like toothpaste) Beautiful designs are made on the Brides hands with the mendi. When the designs are completed the girl must sit for at least two hours or more for the paste to dry and leave the dark red designs on her skin. Older ladies, Grannies and old aunts with white hair finish up the excess mendi by putting it on their white hair, making jokes, saying, when the groom sees them he will fancy them, rather than the young girl. Sweets and fruit are passed around and the jokes continue. When the mendi is declared dry it is removed and perfumed oils are rubbed onto the hands. A yellow paste is rubbed into the brides skin, this gives her a healthy glow, This paste is called holdi. The day ends with the Bride being helped with a bath by her sisters and friends. She is dressed in a yellow sari, even girls who have a darker skin colour take on a golden hue.

Day two - On invitation the Senior ladies of the family go to the Grooms residence to deliver gifts from his father-in-law to be. These are looked over and accepted by the Grooms relatives, then Sweetmeats are eaten and the ladies depart to give full reports of how well they were welcomed. Meanwhile beautification of the Bride continues. Her hair, her nails, body massaged,top to toe perfumed and pampered. Each time she has a bath a full set of new clothes is given to her to wear, each a different colour to denote at what stage the preparations for marriage are at. At no time will she wear white as in the East white is a colour of mourning. She is leaving her old life and entering her new life with happy memories. The wedding day dawns, already the cooks are hard at work having started the previous day with preparing the spices, and making the many sweetmeats. The large cooking pots are by now on the fires,and the animals have been butchered. The cooking starts and the aroma increases as the day goes on.

Like any wedding day the bride is made ready by her friends and family. It is traditional for her to wear red, The marriage sari will be heavily embroidered with silk or gold thread, she will be wearing the jewellery her father has bought her. By about lunch time the family will all be there in their finery. The time of the groom will have been decided and so they wait fro him to come with his relatives.

From a distance you can hear the drums beating, sometimes the Groom will hire a band, and if the Groom is coming by car the horn will be sounded for the last half mile. The Groom makes his arrival as spectacular as possible. I have known grooms to even arrive on a horse or Elephant, if one is available.

The ladies of the Grooms family go inside the house to be with the Brides female relatives and the men stay with the Groom. The children of the Brides family bar the way of the Grooms party,and he and his party are only allowed in after paying a bribe to them. The actual ceremony is very simple, the Bride is asked if she will take this man, then the Groom is asked if he takes this woman. Both must say yes. This is done three times, the Registrar, priest and two witnesses must hear the answers. This is done in two separate areas so after each response the four men have to move to the other one, this can take some time. Then they both sign the Register. Again witnessed by the four men. After that they will sit together on a small platform so that every one can see them. Then the Feasting begins, with music coming out of the speakers on the roof, there is lots of chatter and laughter, it was quite late by the time all the guest depart for their homes. This wedding is of a favourite niece of ours, so we had helped quite a lot with the organisation. Now the sisters, girl cousins and girl friends of Dalim the Bride, sat around her. The Groom is a young engineer working in our Company. They had liked each other for some time, so we had given them a little help towards this happy day. Their friends after some time socialising said ' Good night' and went to bed leaving the newly weds in peace. Tomorrow the happy pair will leave for the Grooms house where the festivities would all start again. This time we will be the guests, there will be lots of feasting and fun which will continue for another two days, at the Grooms house.

Chapter Twenty Three

We had been invited to go to our Farms, which were about ten miles from Khulna. The place we were visiting was by invitation of the Hindu Farmer's wives. Although the men came to see us in our house in Khulna usually Muslims and Christians are not welcome in Hindu homes. The Hindu Farmers after being in refugee camps on the Benapole border during the civil war, had been delighted to get back to their own village.

Starting from scratch, they had to make new houses as everything had been burnt to the ground by the Pakistani Army. We gave them some help, and as they were very good tenant farmers we were happy for them to continue on our land. It took some time, for the crops to grow, but after about two years, again they were getting a good yield of rice, things were nearly back to normal.

Now Lombu would come to see us, as his father had become quite old and Lombu had taken over the care of the extended family.
One day much to my surprise Lombu's father came, not to talk about the farm but to tell us that Lombu was ill. After listening, and having the problem described I thought it would be best for them to bring him to the Khulna District Hospital, and let the Civil Surgeon take a look at Lombu. As he was too ill to even move he had to be carried all the way. This was done by three of his brothers and a friend. The Civil surgeon had to operate immediately. Being village people they really did not wish to stay in the Hospital longer than necessary.

As soon as he was well enough we offered one of our guest rooms to him and his brother, this was a very unusual situation as Hindu's do not stay under the same roof, as non-Hindu's. Lombu's father went back to the village, and as soon as the Patient was well enough to take the journey Lombu went home. We had now been invited by the ladies of the Farming family, these ladies normally stayed at home and only left their Village when they went to India. They wanted us to go so that they could say thank you personally for looking after Lombu.

First we had to take a cycle Rickshaw out of the Town, roads got narrower, and could not take the width of the rickshaw any longer, we left the rickshaw to continued in a little boat, a bit like a Canoe in shape. Between the made up banks of the paddy fields there was water deep enough to take these small craft. Progress was slow and as we only had to go ten miles it took almost to midday before we sighted the village. For the last three hundred yards we had to get out of the boats and cross little streams on bamboo bridges. The locals hop over these bridges with ease but it was quite difficult for us, trying to balance on a thick single bamboo and walk over as if on a tight rope.

The ladies were delighted we had gone to see them, and they had prepared many dishes for us, the Hindu cooking is a little different to the Muslim cooking but, they had taken great care and everything was quite delicious. We ate from earthen dishes, after the meal the dishes would be broken as we were not of their faith, also we had to be very mindful not to touch any of their personal belongings, as they may get upset.

The village children excitedly showed us their school and took us in to the class room. This was a single room with a thatched roof, Rows of wooden benches faced the Blackboard. The sides of this building were open; the floor was made of earth, but they were very proud to show it to us.

Looking out across the surrounding land we could see people working and cows tilling the land, getting the land ready to plant another harvest. Everywhere was lush vegetation and lots of coconut trees and banana plants. Although it must have been quite hot, it did not seem to be as there was a lovely breeze gently coming over the paddy fields.

It seemed a long ten miles back home, we reached Khulna just as the evening prayer was being called; we had experienced very different religions living peacefully side by side.

Chapter Twenty Four

Sitting in the sunshine in Rome, watching the world go by, with a lovely ice cream, we are deciding how we will spend the next days in Italy. We had been to Saudi Arabia staying for just over a week, so that my husband could visit some of the shrines there. After our first day in Saudi Arabia I felt quite overcome with the heat, so my husband had done a trip by himself while I stayed in the hotel. Even in the hotel room I had to wear a veil, room service brought my meals and in the absence of a table the food was laid out for me on the carpet. Later we found out that the locals did not go out until evening time, July is the hottest month in the year. We did go out to see the Shops, that was well into the night when it was much cooler. A strange thing did happen, as we walked along I could hear a persistent hiss just behind me, not understanding I continued walking and looking in shops, it was quite busy, then I realised a man was wishing to pass me. Why not just say 'Excuse me'? It seems as I was wearing a full Burkha, in respect he was asking to pass me, with this hissing sound. When a woman wears the full Burkha there are certain rules to be followed by men. A man cannot speak to a women other than his own wife in Public, so the hiss was his only way to ask permission to pass me. Also he must make sure he has enough room to pass and that his clothing would not touch the lady as this would be a major offence to the lady. What a lot I still had to learn. After this, as soon as I heard a hiss I moved out of the way. I had been given permission from the Saudi Arabian High Commissioner in Dacca to travel in Saudi Arabia so when I felt a little better I visited Mecca. I had special documents in my British Passport with the permission. Certain check posts are on the way with warnings in many languages, with my documents I had no trouble.

The last year had been quite rough for us, Doctors told me to be happy with the three healthy children I had, and not to have any more. I had conceived and decided that I would not terminate the pregnancy. Going to the Holy Family Hospital where I had my other children I felt confident that all would be well. Again I had complications and had to have a Caesarean at eight and a half months, unfortunately I had a heart attack during the delivery and my life was in a balance, it was four days before I understood that I had a baby boy. He was not well, everything was done for him but he was not strong enough to pull through and died when he was one month old. I was still recovering and in hospital, I wanted to go home to Khulna where my children were. Recovery was very slow and after nine months the Doctor advised both of us to take a break. Following this advice we planned to take three months complete break and leaving the family in safe hands and went for our tour of Europe. While in Italy we travelled first up the country to Pisa and saw the leaning Tower, then back to Rome to see all the sights there. We also visited the Vatican. Pope John had died and we were in Rome when the new Pope was elected and we saw the smoke coming from the chimney of the Vatican. After Rome we travelled to Monte Casino and on to Capri, we went through the Blue Grotto on a little boat then stopping at Sorrento on the way back to Rome. Soon our fortnight was up and we had a flight booked for Madrid in Spain. We were beginning to relax.

The Air lines had booked our accommodation at our different stops, when we got to the hotel it looked very grand. The hotel was in Central Madrid overlooking the Kings Palace. What a lovely place to stay. As we were on one of the upper floors we had very good views of Madrid. We found Madrid to be full of life, and so spent most of our time there, we enjoyed the tapas bars very much, we did not drink alcohol but my husband loved his food and Spanish food was very much to his liking. We were now ready to go to England, first we went York to stay with my parents, we were there about three weeks, Mam and Dad had a booked holiday we could have stayed at home in York, but when Nan and Duncan invited us to go to Dumbarton we went up to Scotland to stay with them, by now they had two children Jamie and Jane. We then went down to London and decided that we would like to see Paris so we booked a late afternoon flight. Travelling in a taxi through London and looking for somewhere to eat we saw the BT Tower, the taxi driver told us it was possible to eat in the rotating restaurant up there. We were able to get into the Restaurant and had a wonderful lunch, I remember having Dover Sole. Followed by Crème Brule. During lunch we went around twice, as the Restaurant revolved we had such a wonderful view of London. Getting a taxi straight to the Airport we hopped on the plane to Paris. We were only staying two days, that evening we ate up in the restaurant of the Eiffel Tower, just for the fun of it. I loved Paris and wished we had booked for a longer stay. The rest of our holiday we spent in York. This was the hot Summer of 1976 and during the time we had been in England it had not rained once, we were beginning to wonder if it would rain before we left. At the beginning of October it rained, I had never seen the fields look so dry, and it was the first time I saw policemen without their uniform jackets. As English coinage had gone decimal while I was away, at first it was strange getting to know the new money and also on this visit I saw colour Television for the first time. When we got home to Khulna we had lots to tell them about our wonderful trip.

With my children
Solomon 16 years old
mary 13 years old
Monica 8 Years old

Chapter Twenty Five

The children had grown while we were away but were very pleased to see us back home. We soon got back into the swing of things, with the business and our Social life. The Rotary Club took up a lot of our time. Up to now I had worked in tandem with the men helping the Members of the Rotary Club in their different projects, the ladies were called Rotary Anne's, I thought that we should form The Inner Wheel which is for the ladies and an affiliated organisation to the men. The ladies were very enthusiastic and we formed with me the Founder President.

Our aim was educational opportunities for girls, and vocational training for girls. This was a start, we did some Fund raising and set up a scholarship to enable a girl to continue with her education, this was necessary as when a girl got to a certain age parents would be thinking about her possible marriage, talented girls needed help to stay in Education. My father-in-law was by now into his ninety fifth year, but he took an interest in what I was doing. Always ready with good ideas and advice, He was getting a bit senile, on a good day everything was quite normal but on a bad day it was more difficult, my husband could not cope with the unusual things he did, my girls would prompt him when he got forgetful and frustrated, we all kept an eye on Grandad to keep him happy. After the children had gone to school or college he would join me and sometimes he would be quite childlike in his behaviour. He had always treated me with dignity and so I was always there for him, good day or bad. Some times I would hear gossip regarding my husband, but I trusted him and dismissed it for what it was, Gossip. Well meaning family members also told me things but I still did not believe such stories.

We had hopes of our son going into Engineering, but although he had a brain he was far more interested in Playing Cricket for the local team and missing school to go to the Cinema. He got good grades in his Matriculation Exam but did not want to go to University. This caused some disquiet at home as he was now our only son. His father was very disappointed but he still enrolled our son into the local College.

My father-in-law had a heart attack and after a short illness died he was in his ninety seventh year.

One day early in 1978 my husband announced he needed to go to Germany on business, would I like to go with him as far as England to see my Mam and Dad. For some time Dad had not been very well, He had collapsed while riding his bike, suffering black eyes and a broken nose, and after that the Doctors found he had a heart problem. My husband said we would travel back together. The children would again stay at home as it was only a short trip and they were in the middle of the school year.

Myself with Mam and Dad

I went to see my Mam and Dad, my husband went to Germany, After a few days he was back, much earlier than expected and asking him about the trip he let slip that he had not been alone. He had met up with the Oxford university girl he had met in Bangladesh, and taken her with him as his PA. I was angry. She had then met some of her own friends while they were in Paris and decided that she would go off with them, and had left my husband by him self. We had a good heart to heart talk, I did say that I thought maybe I should stay in England, he promised that things would change, I believed him , also the girls were still young, and needed me, so I went back to Bangladesh with him.

When we got home a bigger shock was waiting for me. I knew that my father-in-law was leaving me some property in his will. He wanted me to continue my Charity work, income from this Inherited property would enable me to be independent of my husbands money. Which was mostly invested in his business. The trip to see my Mam and Dad was a way of getting me out of Bangladesh, so that I would not know that the Will was being challenged by my husband. His lawyer told the court that my father-in-law was of unsound mind and so the will was invalid. Also I was a Foreign National, and I did not live in Bangladesh, spending much of my time abroad. (I had kept my British Passport) The Court decided in my husbands favour. This was all done very hush hush as even my son did not know about it until it was all settled. So everything went to my husband. As my husband was always very generous and I thought we shared every thing my husband explained that it would be better this way.

My husband decided that as our son was now growing in to a young man he should be given some rooms for himself. I thought this was a good idea, but at the same time without mentioning it to me, my husband also moved, out of our apartment into his fathers apartment. This I was told was because the girls were growing into young ladies, so we had men's quarters and ladies quarters in our home. My husband and I were now living apart at home, we still accepted social invitations and attended functions together as we had always done, I was too proud to tell anyone what was happening at home. To outside friends everything was as normal. I still had the beautiful clothes, a large house, and married to a very successful business man. To get me through I put on an act, the girls were young teenagers and I tried my best not to get them involved.

Over the years I had been given a lot of jewellery, not only by my husband, who each Birthday, Christmas and the two Eid's gave me some jewellery, but also family and friends also gave me some lovely gold trinkets. Also I had my mother-in-laws jewellery after she died. Most of my jewellery was now kept in the bank, I could only keep at home what I normally wore every day, which was a gold chain and locket, four gold bangles, gold earrings and a diamond ring, my wedding ring, Eternity ring and my engagement ring. When I wanted money I had to go through the Accountant and Cashier in the office. At first the children would share their pocket money with me. So I started sending some of my goats with Niab Ali a trusted worker, to sell in the Bazaar. When my husband found out, he had the butcher come, and he had all of the goats slaughtered and put into the freezer. I was a prisoner in a Golden Cage. I did have some good friends and they assured me that if I wanted to get out they would help me, I contacted the British High Commission and they told me that, as I had gone to Bangladesh of my own accord, they could do nothing for me. I then decided that I would enjoy the time I had with my children and would go out of my way to fall in with most of my husbands wishes, I aimed for harmony because my time with the family was short, if and when I next went to England I would not be coming back. We went on picnics went shopping and socialised just as normal, but without my husband as most of the time he was too busy with his own pursuits. Being a prominent person in our Area my husband never wished to loose face with his friends and associates, I let it be widely known that I may have to go home at short notice as my father was not well. This was my life line.

When I needed to get out it was one of my friend's husband who brought me a Bangladesh Biman ticket to London, to enable me to fly out the following day.

Landing and safety at Heathrow

Right
Sharashati a Hindu
Lady with her children

Below
Niab Ali, my trusted worker who presented me with flowers on a recent visit to Bangladesh

Epilogue

Things had happened in the last six months I was in Bangladesh to make me frightened for my own safety. My dog had disappeared the day after growling at my husband when he was threatening me.

My husband wanted to marry again as he wanted more children. I couldn't agree with this. I had always turned a blind eye to his friendship with other ladies, the English girl still turned up at our house, usually for a hand out which she always got, then she was on her way again.

Being so far away from home I had to cope with these problems and not involve the children, as the problem was between me and my husband, he was a good provider and good father to them.

A letter came from my Mother asking me to go home as Dad was by now very ill. I said good -bye to the children knowing I would not return. It was difficult.

By this time my husband knew there was every possibility I would not return but, to stop me from going would mean he would loose face with his Rotary friends, who had all rallied round to get me a ticket quickly.

He took my remaining jewellery from me leaving me with my wedding ring. I had no luggage, just the clothes I was wearing my handbag had my passport and nothing else in it. My son gave me a $100 note which quickly went into my bra. Not knowing how I would manage without any source of income I flew to London.

On arrival in London I had a job getting rid of the Airlines hospitality who met me at the airport. We had always travelled with Biman; maybe they saw my name on the passenger list. Changing the dollars into sterling, I purchased a train ticket to York. I was finally home and still in one piece.

First I went to see my Dad who was in hospital, then home with my Mother. She noticed that I had no luggage but thought it would be coming home after me, as it had on other occasions.

Then I told Mam everything. I lived with her while I got myself sorted out.

Not having anything to wear I went to a charity shop and bought some clothes. By this time, after buying new underwear and tights from M & S my money was about finished.

Round-about this time Mam told me about a letter that my husband had written to my parents, telling them I was terminally ill. He had also written to my friends Nan and Duncan with the same story. If I had any doubts before this, I knew returning was not a possibility.

Six weeks after my return my Dad died. I managed to get a job although friend's told me I was unemployable, with no qualifications and having led such a different life up to then, I was able to prove them wrong.

Before my father died I promised him that I would not return to Bangladesh.

My Son wrote to me, telling me that his Father had married again, my husband also wrote asking me to go back (not mentioning his new wife).

After I started Divorce proceedings, my Husband began to harass and threaten me.

He then came to England with the intention of making me go back with him.

I had to take out a court injunction for him to stay away from me and also my Mother. The help of my Brother was invaluable at this time. My brother had just come out of the army and he was in York just when I needed him.

Police protection was not offered to me, I believe in those days it was classed as a 'domestic' although my Husband claimed to have offered £200 to get a contract killer to finish me off.

These treats were heard by my brother, plus we had other proof of threats to do some injury, also abusive letters to my Mother who had just lost my Father, my solicitor was able to give evidence to the court regarding these things. The judge taking all the evidence into consideration then ordered my Husband to leave the country. I was granted an injunction, which stated if I came to any harm from my husband or his agents, my Husband would be held responsible. On the advice of my Solicitor I changed my name by Deed Poll, I got a new job and moved to a different area. Still he contested the Divorce, (knowing I didn't have money) He took it to the High Court, Hiring a top lawyer he challenged and denied everything.

I applied for Legal Aid, which I got. Also by now my Solicitor would not let it go without a fight, she got a Barrister to fight my case. Her office had some very mysterious things happen, and it was thought that my husband may be behind these things.

I knew that I would never get custody of my daughter Monica and found it very difficult to stand in the High Court in Leeds and say I did not want anything from my husband. I told the Court that he was a good father and could provide the girls with everything. I had nothing, if I got the children I could not give them the life they were used to, also I felt that when they were older and not dependent on him they could then decide if they wished to be in contact with me. In Muslim Law it is normal for the children stay with the father. I walked out of the Court with my freedom.

When it was all over I had to pay back the money, to legal Aid. Each monthly installment was a joy. Working and paying back what I owed was therapy. Over the next years very few letters were exchanged between myself and my three children, we were always very careful. I moved down to Surrey, my letters would go to my brother in Northampton by post, Robert would send the letter to my son-in-law Pierre, who was working in Saudi Arabia, he would then pass on the news to the rest of the family. News came back to me by the same method. This was very time consuming so we only exchanged letters about every three months.

My brother moved, and at the same time, a letter went astray which told me that Pierre had a new job, and was going to work in Dubai where Mary would join him. We had lost touch and although I wrote to Pierre at his old address, the letter was returned to me as 'addressee unknown'. after this I had no communication until 2004 when out of the blue my brother Robert brought me a letter. It was more like a note, just saying 'Mammy we are looking for you, if you get this note please make contact'.

Always on my guard, I wondered after all this time, is this a trap? Someone in the Post office was known to my brother and they were able to redirect a letter to my brother's new address. We had been out of contact for about three years. After about a month I replied but with caution, the letter I received was from my daughter Mary who was now living in Dubai. This was the break through we needed, for me to have full contact with my family.

After a few exchanges of letters and phone calls, Mary, Pierre and their son David came to England for a visit. David was the first Grandchild to call me Granny as Joti, my sons little girl, had been a very young baby when I had come to England.

Adrian and I were invited to go to Dubai and spent about a month with them the following winter.

The next summer, Monica came to England with her two little boys, she stayed for most of the summer, her husband Abid came at the end of summer staying for a fortnight, they then went to stay in London where Abid's best friend lived, then went home together.

We went to Bangladesh and stayed with Monica and Abid. Monica lives in a Joint Family. Abid's brothers and their families and also Abid's widowed mother all live in the same building. Abid's sister is married and lives near by. We were able to meet a lot of friends and family on this visit. Often we were stopped by people who remembered me. When in the supermarket, a young lady came up to me to say hello, I had last seen her when she was just a little girl, and her mother had been a very good friend. My TV repair man stopped our Rickshaw to say Hello, and introduce me to his wife and family, When in Bangladesh I feel as if I am among friends, I love Bangladesh and I am lucky to call two countries my home.

David is married and they have a little boy, and live in Dubai. Mary and Pierre, are now retired and live in Bangladesh. Monica's sons are growing up fast; both are doing very well at their schools.

My son rings me on my birthday and the New Year; he always wants to be the first to ring me, with the six hours time difference I get my greetings a little ahead of time. He has quite a large family, I still have not been able to meet some of my grandchildren as they are scattered in other countries. Many of them are married and with children.

We are now a normal family. I enjoy nothing better than to have a chat on the phone, with my girls, which we do each week, more often if we have some special news.

Mary and Pierre

Myself with my sons first daughter, my first grandchild. Joti age 10 months.

Above. Myself with Daughter Monica, her brother-in-law and sister-in-law and my Grandsons Auntu and Mitul.

Left
Myself, Monica and Adrian with Monica's youngest son Mitul

Above.
Adrian and I before we say goodbye to friends and family at the end of our last visit.

Left.
Going for an evening ride with Monica.